"十四五"职业教育国家规划教材

民航客舱实用英语
口语教程（上册）

主　编◎李　姝　李雯艳　韩　黎
副主编◎曹璐璐　刘　君　刘

Practical English Speaking
Course for Aviation Service

（Volume One）

清华大学出版社
北京

内 容 简 介

　　《民航客舱实用英语口语教程(上册)》共计 6 单元。每单元包含核心关键词、热点句型、情景对话和相关文化背景赏析。本书以搭乘航班的基本流程为主线,较翔实地介绍了在机场、机舱及飞行过程中,空乘服务的常用对话、必备经典句型和民航乘务人员职场文化素养常识,包括票务服务、机场服务、登机手续服务、机舱乘务服务、特殊乘客服务、抵达后服务和乘务播音等专业场景。

图书在版编目(CIP)数据

民航客舱实用英语口语教程. 上册:英文 / 李姝,李雯艳,韩黎主编. —北京:清华大学出版社,2018
(2024.9重印)

　　("十三五"全国高等院校民航服务专业规划教材)

　　ISBN 978-7-302-50257-9

　　Ⅰ. ①民… Ⅱ. ①李… ②李… ③韩… Ⅲ. ①民用航空-乘务人员-英语-口语-高等学校-教材 Ⅳ. ①F560.9

　　中国版本图书馆CIP数据核字(2018)第112254号

责任编辑:杜春杰
封面设计:刘　超
版式设计:楠竹文化
责任校对:赵丽杰
责任印制:刘海龙

出版发行:清华大学出版社
　　　　　网　　　址:https://www.tup.com.cn, https://www.wqxuetang.com
　　　　　地　　　址:北京清华大学学研大厦 A 座　　　邮　　编:100084
　　　　　社 总 机:010-83470000　　　　　　　　　邮　　购:010-62786544
　　　　　投稿与读者服务:010-62776969,c-service@tup.tsinghua.edu.cn
　　　　　质量反馈:010-62772015,zhiliang@tup.tsinghua.edu.cn
印 装 者:三河市龙大印装有限公司
经　　销:全国新华书店
开　　本:185mm×260mm　　　印　　张:8.5　　　字　　数:196千字
版　　次:2018 年 6 月第 1 版　　　　　　　　　印　　次:2024 年 9 月第 6 次印刷
定　　价:28.00 元

产品编号:077343-01

"十三五"全国高等院校民航服务专业规划教材编委会

出　版　说　明

随着经济的稳步发展，我国已经进入经济新常态的阶段，特别是十九大指出：中国社会主要矛盾已经转化为人民日益增长的美好生活需要和不平衡不充分的发展之间的矛盾，这客观上要求社会服务系统要完善升级。作为公共交通运输的主要组成部分，民航运输在满足人们对美好生活追求和促进国民经济发展中扮演着重要的角色，具有广阔的发展空间。特别是"十三五"期间，国家高度重视民航业的发展，将民航业作为推动我国经济社会发展的重要战略产业，预示着我国民航业将会有更好、更快的发展。从国产化飞机 C919 的试飞，到宽体飞机规划的出台，以及民航发展战略的实施，标志着我国民航业已经步入崭新的发展阶段，这一阶段的特点是以人才为核心，而这一发展模式必将进一步对民航人才质量提出更高的要求。面对民航业发展对人才培养提出的挑战，培养服务于民航业发展的高质量人才，不仅需要转变人才培养观念，创新教育模式，更需要加强人才培养过程中基本环节的建设，而教材建设就是其首要的任务。

我国民航服务专业的学历教育经过 18 年的探索与发展，其办学水平、办学结构、办学规模、办学条件和师资队伍等方面都发生了巨大的变化，专业建设水平稳步提高，适应民航发展的人才培养体系初步形成。但我们应该清醒地看到，目前我国民航服务类专业的人才培养仍存在着诸多问题，特别是专业人才培养质量仍不能适应民航发展对人才的需求，人才培养的规模与高质量人才短缺的矛盾仍很突出。而目前相关专业教材的开发还处于探索阶段，缺乏系统性与规范性。已出版的民航服务类专业教材，在吸收民航服务类专业研究成果方面做出了有益的尝试，涌现出不同层次的系列教材，推动了民航服务的专业建设与人才培养，但从总体来看，民航服务类教材的建设仍落后于民航业对专业人才培养的实践要求，教材建设已成为相关人才培养的瓶颈。这就需要以引领和服务专业发展为宗旨，系统总结民航服务实践经验与教学研究成果，开发全面反映民航服务职业特点、符合人才培养规律和满足教学需要的系统性专业教材，以积极、有效地推进民航服务专业人才的培养工作。

基于上述思考，编委会经过两年多的实际调研与反复论证，在广泛征询民航业内专家的意见与建议，总结我国民航服务类专业教育的研究成果后，结合我国民航服务业的发展趋势，致力于编写出一套系统的、具有一定权威性和实用性的民航服务类系列教材，为推进我国民航服务人才的培养尽微薄之力。

本系列教材由沈阳航空航天大学、南昌航空大学、郑州航空工业管理学院、上海民航职业技术学院、长沙航空职业技术学院、西安航空职业技术学院、中原工学院、上海外国语大学、山东大学、大连外国语大学、沈阳师范大学、曲阜师范大学、湖南艺术职业学院、陕西师范大学、兰州大学、云南大学、四川大学、湖南民族职业学院、江西青年职业学院、天津交通职业学院、潍坊职业学院、南京旅游职业学院等多所高校的众多资深专家和学者共同打造，还邀请了多名原中国东方航空公司、原中国南方航空公司、原中国国际航空公司和原海南航空公司中从事多年乘务工作的乘务长和乘务员参与教材的编写。

目前，我国民航服务类的专业教育呈现着多元化、多层次的办学格局，各类学校的办学模式也呈现出个性化的特点，在人才培养体系、课程设置以及课程内容等方面，各学校之间存在着一定的差异，对教材也有不同的需求。为了能够更好地满足不同办学层次、教学模式对教材的需要，本套教材主要突出以下特点。

第一，兼顾本、专科不同培养层次的教学需要。鉴于近些年我国本科层次民航服务专业办学规模的不断扩大，在教材需求方面显得十分迫切，同时，专科层面的办学已经到了规模化的阶段，完善与更新教材体系和内容迫在眉睫，本套教材充分考虑了各类办学层次的需要，本着"求同存异、个性单列、内容升级"的原则，通过教材体系的科学架构和教材内容的层次化，以达到兼顾民航服务类本、专科不同层次教学之需要。

第二，将最新实践经验和专业研究成果融入教材。服务类人才培养是系统性问题，具有很强的内在规定性，民航服务的实践经验和专业建设成果是教材的基础，本套教材以丰富理论、培养技能为主，力求夯实服务基础、培养服务职业素质，将实践层面行之有效的经验与民航服务类人才培养规律的研究成果有效融合，以提高教材对人才培养的有效性。

第三，落实素质教育理念，注重服务人才培养。习近平总书记在党的十九大报告中强调，"要全面贯彻党的教育方针，落实立德树人根本任务，发展素质教育，推进教育公平，培养德智体美全面发展的社会主义建设者和接班人"，人才以德为先，以社会主义价值观铸就人的灵魂，才能使人才担当重任，也是高校人才培养的基本任务。教育实践表明，素质是人才培养的基础，也是人才职业发展的基石，人才的能力与技能以精神与灵魂为附着，但在传统的民航服务教材体系中，包含素质教育板块的教材较为少见。根据党的教育方针，本套教材的编写考虑到素质教育与专业能力培养的关系，以及素质对职业生涯的潜在影响，首次在我国民航服务专业教学中提出专业教育与人文素质并重，素质决定能力的培养理念，以独特的视野精心打造素质教育教材板块，使教材体系更加系统，强化了教材特色。

第四，必要的服务理论与专业能力培养并重。调研分析表明，忽视服务理论与人文素质所培养出的人才很难有宽阔的职业胸怀与职业精神，其未来的职业生涯发展就会乏力。因此，教材不应仅是对单纯技能的阐述与训练指导，更应该是不淡化专业能力培养的同时，强化行业知识、职业情感、服务机理、职业道德等关系到职业发展潜力的要素的培养，以期培养出高层次和高质量的民航服务人才。

第五，架构适合未来发展需要的课程体系与内容。民航服务具有很强的国际化特点，而我国民航服务的思想、模式与方法也正处于不断创新的阶段，紧紧把握未来民航服务的发展趋势，提出面向未来的解决问题的方案，是本套教材的基本出发点和应该承担的责任。我们力图将未来民航服务的发展趋势、服务思想、服务模式创新、服务理论体系以及服务管理等内容进行重新架构，以期能对我国民航服务人才培养，乃至整个民航服务业的发展起到引领作用。

第六，扩大教材的种类，使教材的选择更加宽泛。鉴于我国目前尚缺乏民航服务专业更高层次办学模式的规范，各学校的人才培养方案各具特点，差异明显，为了使教材更适合于办学的需要，本套教材打破了传统教材的格局，通过课程分割、内容优化和课外外延化等方式，增加了教材体系的课程覆盖面，使不同办学层次、关联专业，可以通过教材合理组合获得完整的专业教材选择机会。

本套教材规划出版品种大约为四十种，分为：① 人文素养类教材，包括《大学语文》《应用文写作》《艺术素养》《跨文化沟通》《民航职业修养》《中国传统文化》等。② 语言类教材，包括《民航客舱服务英语教程》《民航客舱实用英语口语教程》《民航实用英语听力教程》《民航播音训练》《机上广播英语》《民航服务沟通技巧》等。③ 专业类教材，包括《民航概论》《民航服务概论》《中国民航常飞客源国概况》《民航危险品运输》《客舱安全管理与应急处置》《民航安全检查技术》《民航服务心理学》《航空运输地理》《民航服务法律实务与案例教程》等。④ 职业形象类教材，包括《空乘人员形体与仪态》《空乘人员职业形象设计与化妆》《民航体能训练》等。⑤ 专业特色类教材，包括《民航服务手语训练》《空乘服务专业导论》《空乘人员求职应聘面试指南》《民航面试英语教程》等。

为了开发职业能力，编者联合有关 VR 开发公司开发了一些与教材配套的手机移动端 VR 互动资源，学生可以利用这些资源体验真实场景。

本套教材是迄今为止民航服务类专业较为完整的教材系列之一，希望能借此为我国民航服务人才的培养，乃至我国民航服务水平的提高贡献力量。民航发展方兴未艾，民航教育任重道远，为民航服务事业发展培养高质量的人才是各类人才培养部门的共同责任，相信集民航教育的业内学者、专家之共同智慧，凝聚有识之士心血的这套教材的出版，对加速我国民航服务专业建设、完善人才培养模式、优化课程体系、丰富教学内容，以及加强师资队伍建设能起到一定的推动作用。在教材使用的过程中，我们真诚地希望听到业内专家、学者批评的声音，收到广大师生的反馈意见，以利于进一步提高教材的水平。

客服信箱：thjdservice@126.com。

丛 书 序

《礼记·学记》曰："古之王者，建国君民，教学为先。"教育是兴国安邦之本，决定着人类的今天，也决定着人类的未来，企业发展也大同小异，重视人才是企业的成功之道，别无二选。航空经济是现代经济发展的新趋势，是当今世界经济发展的新引擎，民航是经济全球化的主流形态和主导模式，是区域经济发展和产业升级的驱动力。作为发展中的中国民航业，有巨大的发展潜力，其民航发展战略的实施必将成为我国未来经济发展的增长点。

"十三五"期间正值实现我国民航强国战略构想的关键时期，"一带一路"倡议方兴未艾，"空中丝路"越来越宽阔。面对高速发展的民航运输，需要推动持续的创新与变革；同时，基于民航运输的安全性和规范性的特点，其对人才有着近乎苛刻的要求，只有人才培养先行，夯实人才基础，才能抓住国家战略转型与产业升级的巨大机遇，实现民航运输发展的战略目标。经过多年民航服务人才发展的积累，我国建立了较为完善的民航服务人才培养体系，培养了大量服务民航发展的各类人才，保证了我国民航运输业的高速持续发展。与此同时，我国民航人才培养正面临新的挑战，既要通过教育创新，提升人才品质，又需要在人才培养过程中精细化，把人才培养目标落实到人才培养的过程中，而教材作为专业人才培养的基础，需要先行，从而发挥引领作用。教材建设发挥的作用并不局限于专业教育本身，其对行业发展的引领，专业人才的培养方向，人才素质、知识、能力结构的塑造以及职业发展潜力的培养具有不可替代的作用。

我国民航运输发展的实践表明，人才培养决定着民航发展的水平，而民航人才的培养需要社会各方面的共同努力。我们惊喜地看到，清华大学出版社秉承"自强不息，厚德载物"的人文精神，发挥强势的品牌优势，投身到民航服务专业系列教材的开发行列，改变了民航服务教材研发的格局，体现了其对社会责任的担当。

本套教材体系组织严谨，精心策划，高屋建瓴，深入浅出，具有突出的特色。第一，从民航服务人才培养的全局出发，关注了民航服务产业的未来发展趋势，架构了以培养目标为导向的教材体系与内容结构，比较全面地反映了服务人才培养趋势，具有良好的统领性；第二，很好地回归了教材的本质——适用性，体现在每本教材均有独特的视角和编写立意，既有高度的提升、理论的升华，也注重教育要素在课程体系中的细化，具有较强的可用性；第三，引入了职业素质教育的理念，补齐了服务人才素质教育缺少教材的短板，可谓是对传统服务人才培养理念的一次冲击；第四，教材编写人员参与面非常广泛。这反映出本套教材充分体现了当今民航服务专业教育的教学成果和编写者的思考，形成了相互交流的良性机制，势必对全国民航服务类专业的发展起到推动作用。

　　教材建设是专业人才培养的基础，与其服务的行业的发展交互作用，共同实现人才培养—社会检验的良性循环是助推民航服务人才的动力。希望这套教材能够在民航服务类专业人才培养的实践中，发挥更广泛的积极作用。相信通过不断总结与完善，这套教材一定会成为具有自身特色的、适应我国民航业发展要求的，以及深受读者喜欢的规范教材。

　　此为序。

原海南航空公司总裁、原中国货运航空公司总裁、原上海航空公司总裁

朱益民

2017 年 9 月

前　言

　　高质量空乘服务人才的培养需要建立在科学的培养模式、学科建设、规范的课程体系、合理的课程内容与有效的教学方法的基础上。本书是空乘英语在乘务职场中的语言、语境及文化内涵对准空乘人员综合素质能力提升的立体化实用教材。本书力图在教材的科学性、前瞻性和实用性方面有所创新，这使得本书在未来的专业建设与人才培养方面发挥更大的作用。

　　本书是专门为空中乘务、民航服务、空中商务专业的学生以及有志于从事航空服务工作的学习者量身打造的空乘英语口语教材，内容涉及机场、机舱乘务职场领域，是依据工作流程较为人性化的配有语言语境及文化背景的空乘专业英语教材。每单元包含的内容有：核心关键词、热点句型、情景对话和相关文化背景赏析等。本书内容以搭乘航班的基本流程为主线，较翔实地介绍了在机场、机舱及飞行过程中空乘服务的常用对话及必备经典句型和民航乘务人员职场文化素养的背景常识。

　　本着实用为主，适用为度的原则，从听、说、读、写、译等方面全方位培养学生的英语能力与水平，正是本书的编写原则与宗旨。

编　者

2018 年 2 月

CONTEN^{TS} 目录

Unit 1
Booking Service

1.1 Telephone Booking Service

1.1.1 Language Points and Useful Sentence Patterns

1.1.1.1 Language Points

1. available

Obtainable, convenient, ready, at hand, handy.

2. red-eye flight

A night flight from which the passengers emerge with eyes red for a lack of sleep.

3. connecting flight

A flight with an intermediate stop and a change of aircraft (possibly a change of airlines).

4. departure time

The time at which a plane is scheduled to depart from a given point of origin.

5. reservation

If you make a reservation, you arrange for something such as a table in a restaurant or a room in a hotel or a ticket for a flight.

6. direct flight

A flight with one or more intermediate stops but no change of aircraft.

7. nonstop flight

A nonstop flight is one with no intermediate stops.

8. mileage

Mileage refers to the distance that you have travelled, measured in miles.

9. Pearl Miles Silver

China Southern Airlines' frequent flyer program. The program also includes Pearl Miles Ordinary and Gold.

10. valid

Something that is valid is important or serious enough to make it worth saying or doing.

11. refund

A refund is a sum of money which is returned to you, for example because you have paid too much or you have returned something to someplace.

1.1.1.2 Useful Sentence Patterns

1. Greeting

Hello!

Good morning / afternoon / evening!

How are you?

Hi! Love!

Nice / Glad / Pleased to see you.

Replies

I'm OK / fine / all right / very well.

Wonderful!

Couldn't be better!

I'm in a good mood today.

So-so.

Terrible!

I'm under the weather today.

I'm not myself today.

2. Starting a Conversation

Excuse me.

Good morning.

I beg your pardon.

I'm sorry to interrupt you…

Could you tell me…?

Can you spare me a few minutes?

Nice day, isn't it?

You know?

Can you hear that?

1.1.2 Dialogues

1.1.2.1 Booking an Economy Flight

(T: Ticket Clerk   C: Client)

T: Hello, Delta Airlines, good morning. May I help you?

C: Yes, do you have any flights to Wellington next Tuesday afternoon?

T: One moment, Sir. I'll check...Two flights available that afternoon. One departs at 2:45 p.m., the other one is a red-eye flight at 10:00 p.m. Which one do you like, Sir?

C: Hmm...I'd like a regular one, the 2:45 please.

T: Yes, Sir. It is a connecting flight via Sydney.

C: That's fine. Could you tell me how much it costs?

T: Which class do you prefer?

C: Economy, please.

T: That would be $268.

C: OK. Could you help me make a reservation?

T: Certainly, your name please?

C: My name is Jack Smith, that's J-A-C-K-S-M-I-T-H.

T: Now you have been booked, Mr. Smith. The departure time is 2:45 p.m., and your arrival in Wellington will be at 9:55 p.m., local time. The flight number is DL 476.

C: Thank you.

1.1.2.2　Booking a Nonstop Flight

(T: Ticket Clerk　C: Client)

T: China Southern Airline Booking Office. May I help you?

C: I'd like to make a reservation to Guiyang.

T: When would you like to go?

C: The last Friday of this month. I think it's April 28th.

T: We have a flight leaving for Guiyang via Luoyang at 18:35 p.m. Is that OK?

C: Oh. Do you have a direct flight to Guiyang in the morning?

T: One moment, please...Yes, we have a nonstop flight at 7:30 a.m.

C: That's it. Oh, can you please add this to my mileage, please? I'm using Pearl Miles Silver.

T: With pleasure, Sir. Please tell me your membership ID.

C: It is...

T: I've added it. It will be valid if no refund occurs.

C: Great. Thank you. Can I reserve a seat now?

T: Absolutely, Sir. Your name, please?

…

1.1.3　Cultural Background

Boeing

Boeing is the world's largest aerospace company and leading manufacturer of commercial jetliners and defense, space and security systems. A top U.S. exporter, the company supports airlines and U.S. and allied government customers in 150 countries. Boeing products and tailored services include commercial and military aircraft, satellites, weapons, electronic and defense systems, launch systems, advanced information and communication systems, and performance-based logistics and training.

Boeing has been the premier manufacturer of commercial jetliners for more than 40 years. With the merger of Boeing and McDonnell Douglas in 1997, Boeing's leadership in commercial jets, joined with the lineage of Douglas airplanes, gives the combined company a 70-year heritage of leadership in commercial aviation. Today, the main commercial products are the

737,747,767 and 777 families of airplanes and the Boeing Business Jet. New product development efforts are focused on the Boeing 787 Dream-liner, and the 747-8. The company has nearly 12,000 commercial jetliners in service worldwide, which is roughly 75 percent of the world fleet. Through Boeing Commercial Aviation Services, the company provides unsurpassed, around-the-clock technical support to help operators maintain their airplanes in peak operating condition. Commercial Aviation Services offers a full range of world-class engineering, modification, logistics and information services to its global customer base, which includes the world's passenger and cargo airlines, as well as maintenance, repair and overhaul facilities. Boeing also trains maintenance and flight crews in the 100-seat-and-above airliner market through Boeing Training & Flight Services, the world's largest and most comprehensive provider of airline training.

(Data from: http://www.boeing.com)

1.2   Confirming Flight

1.2.1   Language Points and Useful Sentence Patterns

1.2.1.1   Language Points

1. pressing

A pressing problem, need, or issue has to be dealt with immediately.

2. airfare

The airfare to a place is the amount it costs to fly there.

3. first class

The most expensive accommodations on a ship or train or plane.

4. business class

Business class seating on an aeroplane costs less than first class but more than economy class.

5. round trip ticket

If you make a round trip, you travel to a place and then back again.

6. open ticket

An open ticket means you have not decided the departure date, you need to confirm that before your intending fly.

7. regular flight

A regular flight is one departs at the same time for each day.

8. economy class

On an aeroplane, an economy class ticket or seat is the cheapest available.

1.2.1.2　Useful Sentence Patterns

Asking for help

Would you help me with my…?

Could you give me a hand?

Could you do me a favor?

Would you be willing to…?

If it's not too much trouble, I'd appreciate it if you'd…?

Would you be good enough to help me support this old man to the lavatory?

I'd be grateful if you would help me.

Would I be troubling you too much if I asked you to…?

Replies

Of course.

With pleasure.

Certainly I'll do all I can.

Sure, I'll be glad to.

By all means.

I will if I can.

Unfortunately…

I'm sorry. I don't think I can manage it.

I'm afraid I won't be able to.

I'd love to, but I'm afraid I can't.

1.2.2　Dialogues

1.2.2.1　How do you spell it?

(C: Clerk　P: Passenger)

Setting: John calls China Eastern Airlines' Booking Office to check the seat availability. The clerk helps him to book a ticket to Hangzhou the day after tomorrow.

C: Hello, this is China Eastern Airlines' Booking Office. May I help you?

P: Yes, I want to have a ticket to Hangzhou the day after tomorrow. Time is pressing, I'm afraid.

C: I think that should not be a problem. We're not too full at this time of the year. Just a moment, please and I'll check my computer…Thank you for your waiting. Yes, seats are available on MU 3742 on April 8th, the day after tomorrow. But we have no discount on the airfare because the date is nearby.

P: Thank goodness. That's great, may I know the departure time?

C: It is a nonstop flight leaves Shenyang at 8:50 a.m.

P: Okay, MU3742 suits me all right. I'll book that. Make that a first class seat, please.

C: Sorry, Sir. Only business class seat is available.

P: It's better than nothing. I'll take this one.

C: All right, Sir. That's MU3742 on April 8th, the day after tomorrow, one business class seat, to Hangzhou.

P: Yes, that's right.

C: Thank you. Would you spell your family name, please?

P: It's W-I-L-S-O-N.

C: Is that "W" as in William, "I" as in India, "L" as in Larry, "S" as in Sam , "O" as in Ocean, "N" as in Nancy?

P: That's correct.

C: Thank you. Would you please spell your first name?

P: J-O-H-N.

C: Thank you, Mr. Wilson, May I have a telephone number, and where can we contact you?

P: Yes, I'm working in Shenyang Aircraft Manufacturing Company. I stay in 211 of Administration Building. My cell is ...

C: Thank you. Is there anything else I can do for you, Sir?

P: No, that's all. Thank you.

C: Thank you for flying with China Eastern. Have a nice trip.

1.2.2.2 Have you reconfirmed your reservation?

(A: Attendant   J: John)

Setting: John has made a reservation for a flight to Shanghai, and he calls the Booking Office of Delta Airlines to confirm his reservation.

A: Good afternoon, Delta Airlines' ticket office. May I help you?

J: Good afternoon. I booked a round trip ticket with the return open and my travel agent told me that I should confirm the ticket before I fly. I'd like to confirm my flight number, please?

A: Yes, the airlines requires the passengers to confirm their open tickets 72 hours before their intend traveling. Would you like to confirm your tickets now?

J: Yes, please.

A: May I know your flight number, please?

J: It's flight DL 1687, which leaves Rome to Shanghai at 14:40 on November 26th, local time.

A: Oh, yes. DL 1687 is our regular flight to Shanghai. Would you please tell me your name?

J: My name is John Wilson.

A: Yes, Mr. Wilson, here you are. You're flying in economy class. Is that right?

J: Yes, that's it. And I plan to return on December 10th, do you have any tickets available on that day?

A: Let me check. Yes, we have DL 1688 leaves Shanghai at 11:30 a.m. on that day.

J: Fine, make an economy class as well please.

A: Okay. Now, your ticket is in order. Thank you for calling to confirm.

J: It's better to confirm after ordering, right? And I don't want to lose it.

A: Quite right. If you hadn't confirmed, it would be cancelled within 24 hours before the departure time. Have a nice trip, Mr. Wilson.

J: Thank you, Bye.

1.2.3　Cultural Background

Online Tickets Booking

Some decades ago, most people purchase their tickets at the ticket counter. Nowadays most people want to make their flight reservations by telephoning an airline reservations office. But still, our young people would like to book their tickets online. Are you one of those persons, who are afraid of buying plane tickets online, and would rather call the airlines and talk to a "real person"? It is easy to understand that the airlines are encouraging us to buy a ticket online rather than over the phone, because it can save them time and money and they can give the benefits back to the customers. Booking online can be easy and convenient, if you get used to it.

First you need to determine your destination and the departure date, or you just go window shopping to search some special fare. Then you have to figure out whether you are traveling alone or with other people. Next you'd better find out which class of service you desires, the food service, baggage allowance or other special services that an airline can provide.

Start searching as early as possible so that you can take advantage of advance-booking fare. You can use some APP for help. Or you can key in a keyword "cheap plane tickets", it will search for dozens of well-known websites. These websites are fairly straightforward to use—you key in your destination, dates and number of passengers. After a few seconds' wait, you have your results on the screen in front of you. Look for flights on your frequent-flier carrier first and compare its cheapest rate to those on sites. Many airline websites offer lower internet-only fares. The cheapest flight option is usually displayed first at the top of the screen with successive options ranging in price.

Besides price, you may want to consider other aspects too. Such as, request your seat preference, window or aisle, front or back; request any special assistance or equipment, baby cradle, wheelchair or something; request the special meals, Hindus, baby, low-protein or vegetarian meals, and make sure whether they need to be paid or not.

All of these have done, then you can "sure" your order and wait for your wonderful trip.

1.3   Refunding Ticket

1.3.1   Language Points and Useful Sentence Patterns

1.3.1.1   Language Points

1. urgent

If something is urgent, it needs to be dealt with as soon as possible.

2. CAAC

Civil Aviation Administration of China.

3. original fare

The original fare means you spend how much money on your ticket.

4. receipt

A receipt is a piece of paper that you get from someone as proof that they have received money or goods from you.

5. special fare

The special fare is much more cheaper than original fare, and usually has quantity limitation.

6. finals

In a series of events, things, exams, competitions, or people, the final one is the last one.

7. internet-only

The tickets, things, vouchers or the others things you can only purchase online.

1.3.1.2   Useful Sentence Patterns

Offering Help

May I help you with…?

Can I give you a hand?

Would you like me to…?

May I be of any assistance?

Here, let me help you.

Wouldn't you like to have me help…?

Is there anything I can do for you?

If you like, we'd be happy to…

You know, it wouldn't be any trouble for me to do that.

You shouldn't be doing that! Let me…

Replies

Thank you very much.

Great! / Terrific!

Yes, please. Just what I need.

It's very thoughtful of you.

I'd be glad to have your help.

Yes, please, if you don't mind.

Sure, if it's no trouble.

Thanks ever so much, but it's all right, really.

No, thanks. I can do it myself.

Please don't bother about that.

1.3.2 Dialogues

1.3.2.1 Should I have to pay for the refund?

(A: Attendant   P: Passenger)

Setting: Right before Helen's departure, she changes her plan due to some financial matters at her company. Now she is at the reception desk.

A: Good afternoon. Anything I can do for you?

P: Good afternoon, Miss. I have bought a ticket on flight CA829, flying to Paris at 3:25 p.m. this afternoon. But I have something more important to do and I have to stay here for a few more days. Could you please help me get a refund for the ticket? It is very urgent.

A: OK, Miss, may I have your name?

P: Helen Zhang. Should I have to pay for the refund?

A: Yes, you have to pay RMB1,140.

P: Oh, so much? Would you please tell me more about it?

A: Yes, Miss. According to CAAC's regulation, if a passenger (except a group passenger) asks for a refund of his ticket within 24 hours and 2 hours before the departure time, he has to pay 20% of the original fare.

P: What about the other situations? I mean, 24 hours before departure, or within 2 hours?

A: That will be 10% and 50% respectively.

P: Thanks for your information. Here is my ticket and the money for the refund.

A: It's my pleasure to stand with you. Do you need to book another ticket?

P: No, thanks, I have not decided the departure date.

A: Okay. Here is your receipt. See you, Miss.

1.3.2.2 You cannot refund the special fare

(A: Attendant   P: Passenger)

Setting: Mia had some problems about the ticket refund online. Now she is calling Air China.

A: Good morning, Air China Booking Office. Anything I can do for you?

P: Good morning, Miss. I have bought a ticket on your website, from Shenyang to Shenzhen on June 19th. But at that time I can not finish my finals and I have to stay at school for a few more days. I plan to cancel the ticket, but it failed, I don't understand what is going on?

A: OK, Miss, may I have your name?

P: Mia Haywood.

A: And your flight number?

P: CA1782, a morning flight, at 8:05.

A: Yes, Miss. I see. You booked a ticket on that flight a month ago, and got enough our internet-only special fare. According to Air China's regulation, you can not refund the special fare if a passenger books his ticket online.

P: What do you mean? Then what should I do?

A: That is to say, you have to buy another ticket. And this one, unfortunately, if you can not board on time, is invalid.

P: Okay, then I think I should talk to my professor to check whether I can finish my finals earlier. Anyway, I don't want to waste my money.

A: I understand, if there is anything we can do for you, please let me know.

P: Thank you.

1.3.3　Cultural Background

My Daily Life

Any one wants to be a flight attendant? Do you know what I am going to do under my dreaming uniforms? Let me tell you how busy and tough my work is.

1:30 a.m. Good night or good morning?

My cell is ringing…already…and it's time to get up for my flight to Vancouver, which is ready to leave 4 hours later. I get ready for my make-up, my uniform and make sure my passport and regular papers are in my carry-on bag. Several bread in stomach and I catch the staff shuttle bus to the briefing room.

3:45 a.m. Fifteen minutes to the pre-flight briefing

I still got some time to check my cabin crew manual to refresh my knowledge of the all important emergency procedures and location of the emergency equipment and exits for today's aircraft, an Airbus 380.

4:00 a.m. The pre-flight briefing

As usual, today's briefing is held by the senior crew, of course the captain is there too. They make us introduce ourselves and talk to us about the flight details, including the order of the services, the individual positions and responsibilities for the day, and any special points or passengers with special needs. Security and the aircraft's safety features always need to pay special attention and we sometimes ask one or two questions about emergency procedures. This is to make sure the safety of the aircraft and all the passengers.

4:30 a.m. Pre-flight preparations for boarding

This is checking time! My team are going to check the emergency equipment and whether there's a safety instruction card in every passenger's seat pocket. Then we double-check the number of meals on board, the drinks trolley and duty-free goods and stock all the toilets with necessary hand towels and tissues.

5:00 a.m. Welcoming passengers

It is a new day for me, and actually I have prepared 4 hours for this NEW day. This is my responsibilities to make every passenger feel like coming back home and the cabin is their portable home.

1.4 Changing the Date of the Flight

1.4.1 Language Points and Useful Sentence Patterns

1.4.1.1 Language Points

1. one-way ticket

You purchase one-way ticket from one place to another and have no plan to come back.

2. guide dog

A guide dog is a dog that has been trained to lead a blind person.

3. vaccination card

If a person or animal is vaccinated, they are given a vaccine, usually by injection, to prevent them from getting a disease.

4. health certificate

A paper or some documents that shows your body, or your pet's body is healthy.

5. aisle seat

An aisle seat is the seat by the aisle, there is window seat as well.

6. cabin door

We go in and out the cabin by entry cabin door, the FA welcome and see off the passengers at the cabin door.

7. baby meal

A cabin meal for babies, usually including baby rice powder, porridge or something easy for babies to digest.

8. boarding pass

A pass that allows you to board a ship or plane.

1.4.1.2　Useful Sentence Patterns

1. Introducing yourself to someone you do not know

My name's Paola. Pleased to meet you.

Hi there, I'm Tom.

I'm Brown, nice to meet you.

2. Finding out someone's name

May I know your name?

Sorry, what's your name?

Excuse me, could you tell me your name, please?

3. Introducing other people

This is my wife, Kathy Lao.

This is my colleague, Katrin.

This is Hemal.

4. Saying hello to people you know or have met before

Hello again, how are you? Fine thanks. And you?

How's it going? Very well, thanks.

How are you? Not too bad.

Hi there! Hi!

5. Checking and clarifying

Can I just check what the flight time is?

Can you confirm that your crew is familiar with the cockpit procedures?

Can I clarify something?

Can I clarify the time of the meals service?

1.4.2　Dialogues

1.4.2.1　What is the New Date?

(A: Attendant　P: Passenger)

A: Good morning, Spring Airlines Booking Office. What can I do for you?

P: Good morning, Sir. I booked a one-way ticket to Beijing which leaves Sanya on June 20th, and I wonder if I can travel with my dog?

A: Can I ask that is it a guide dog?

P: No, it is a pet dog, but it's not super-sized, a small one.

A: Sir, do you have the health and vaccination card for your pet?

P: Oh, are those things necessary? My dog is gentle and quiet, and I don't think it will disturb others.

A: Yes, Sir. I understand, but according to our rules, you have to deal with your dog's health certificate and vaccination card, and it should be travelled as cargo because it's not a service dog.

P: Then what is your suggestion?

A: I am sorry to say that you'd better change your flight date.

P: How long will it take me to apply for those documents? Would you recommend me the new date? And do I need to pay for the change?

A: One week or so, that is after June 27th. It is free if you change your date before departure.

P: Thank you. Book an aisle seat for me, better near the cabin door, please. I am eager to see my little baby after landing.

A: So your flight is 9C5534 from Sanya to Beijing on June 29th, 5D, an aisle, economy class.

P: OK, thank you.

1.4.2.2　Upgrading to the first class

(A: Attendant　P: Passenger)

P: Good morning, Sir. Here is my passport.

A: Good morning, Sir. You are flying with British Airways from London to Milan.

P: Yes, and can I upgrade my economy class ticket to business class?

A: One moment, Sir....I'm afraid the business class is fully booked now. How about the first class?

P: Oh, would you please check my mileage. I don't think my mile can upgrade me into first class.

A: OK. Let me see, yes, there is enough mile.

P: Great. Please help me with that. By the way, if I am travelling with my 1-year-old daughter, should I buy a ticket for her?

A: Yes, Sir. You should pay 10% of the overhead price if she does not take a seat.

P: All right. May I ask a baby meal for my girl?

A: Of course. We can make a note for you.

P: It's really kind of you. I will try next time.

A: Have a nice day, Sir. Here is your passport and boarding pass.

1.4.3　Cultural Background

Airbus

Airbus is the world's leading aircraft manufacturer whose customer focus, commercial know-how, technological leadership and manufacturing efficiency have propelled it to the forefront of the industry.

Airbus' modern and comprehensive product line comprises highly successful families of aircraft ranging from 107 to 525 seats: the single-aisle A320 Family, the wide-body long-range

A330/A340 and the all-new next generation A350 XWB Family, and the ultra long-range, double-decker A380 Family. The company also continues to broaden its scope and product range by applying its expertise to the military market. It is as well extending its portfolio of freighter aircraft that will set new standards in the general and express freight market sectors.

Across all its fly-by-wire aircraft families Airbus' unique approach ensures that aircraft share the highest possible degree of commonality in airframes, on-board systems, cockpits and handing characteristics, which reduces significantly operating costs for airlines.

Dedicated to helping airlines enhance the profitability of their fleets, Airbus also delivers a wide range of customer services in all areas of support, tailored to the needs of individual operators all over the world.

Headquartered to helping airlines enhance the profitability of their fleets, Airbus also delivers a wide range of customer services in all areas of support, tailored to the needs of individual operators all over the world.

1.5　Waiting List

1.5.1　Language Points and Useful Sentence Patterns

1.5.1.1　Language Points

1. waiting list

A waiting list is a list of people who have asked for something which cannot be given to them immediately, for example medical treatment, housing, or training, and who must therefore wait until it is available.

2. ASAP

Short term of as soon as possible abbreviations.

3. half-fare ticket

50% off the full fare ticket, children above 2 and under 14 needs to buy half-fare ticket.

4. check in counter

At an airport, a check-in is the counter or desk where you check in.

5. UM

Short term of Unaccompanied Minors, children who travel without anyone to look after them. (Children under 14 must be accompanied by an adult.)

1.5.1.2　Useful Sentence Patterns

Asking for Permission

May I put it here?

May I interrupt you?

Do you mind if I take it away?

May I have permission to...?

Would you allow me to...?

You don't mind if I put down the shade, do you?

I wonder if I could put the bags on yours.

Would it be possible to exchange your seat with his?

Replies

Go ahead.

That's OK.

Of course, you may / can.

By all means.

Yes, I suppose so.

I'm sorry, I'm afraid you can't.

I'd prefer you not to...

I'd like to say yes, but it's just not possible.

We don't permit anyone to...

No, please don't...

1.5.2　Dialogues

1.5.2.1　Can I put you on the waiting list?

(T: Ticket Clerk　C: Client)

T: China Eastern Booking Office, may I help you?

C: I need a one-way ticket from Shanghai to Guangzhou, please.

T: May I have your name, please?

C: Sure, Wang Hua. I plan to go with my ten-year-old nephew.

T: Let me see… When do you want to take your departure, Mr. Wang?

C: Next Monday.

T: That is April 17th, to Guangzhou. Sorry, Sir, all seats have been booked. How about next Friday?

C: I'm afraid that will be too late.

T: Then can I put you on the waiting list?

C: What do you mean by that?

T: It means if someone cancels his flight on next Monday, I will give you a call.

C: If there is no other choice, I'll have to accept it.

T: Then please give me your phone number.

C: 136××××××××. Contact me as soon as possible, OK?

T: I will, Sir. I will let you know ASAP. Thank you for flying with China Eastern.

C: Thank you for your help. Bye!

T: Goodbye and have a nice day!

1.5.2.2   Can you put me on the earliest flight for the day after tomorrow?

(T: Ticket Clerk   C: Client)

T: China Eastern Booking Office, may I help you?

C: Morning, Miss. This is Wang Hua. Just now you put me on the waiting list, from Shanghai to Guangzhou, April 17th.

T: Yes, Sir. What is the matter?

C: Can you please put me on the earliest flight for the day after tomorrow?

T: Let me see… Our morning flight is 6:00 a.m. Can this one be OK?

C: OK. Only one ticket please, my nephew travels alone.

T: Children above 2 and younger than 14 should buy a half-fare ticket.

C: I see.

T: You have to fill in a form with details at the check in counter, such as the destination, the contact number, who is going to pick him up at the airport, your nephew will be treated as an UM.

C: Sure, if I can send my son on board. After all, there is no seat available.

T: Everything is in the order. If someone cancels his flight the day after tomorrow, I will give you a call. Is your number $136\times\times\times\times\times\times\times\times$?

C: That's right. Thank you for your help. Bye!

T: Goodbye and have a nice day!

1.5.3   Cultural Background

Sky team and Sky Pearl Club

Aero Mexico, Air France, Delta Airlines and Korean Air founded Sky Team in June 2000. Since then, they have steadily grown to current membership of 19.

Over the last decade—a challenging one for the aviation industry—they have more than tripled their number of member airlines, doubled the number of flights and nearly doubled their destinations, offering their customers easier connections around the world.

So far, there are 19 Sky Team member airlines that make it possible to travel around the world. There are nearly 15,000 daily flights to over 1,000 destinations in 187 countries.

As they have grown, they have continued to offer their customers Frequent Flyer Programs, more destinations, more frequencies and better connectivity. If passengers join the Frequent Flyer Program of any Sky Team member airline and they'll earn frequent flyer miles towards Elite status. The more you fly, the quicker you'll enjoy Priority Chick-in, Preferred Seating and

Lounge Access.

China Southern Airlines joined Sky Team in 2007.

The largest and most popular Frequent Flyer Program in China, China Southern Airlines' Sky Pearl Club offer passengers the fastest way to earn free trips on China's largest airline-as well as special benefits from global airline and commercial partners. Today, the club has more than 13 million members.

Unit 2
Airport Service

2.1 Finding the Direction at the Airport

2.1.1 Language Points and Useful Sentence Patterns

2.1.1.1 Language Points

1. passport

Your passport is an official document containing your name, photograph, and personal details, which you need to show when you enter or leave a country.

2. window seat

On a train, bus, or aeroplane, a window seat is a seat next to a window.

3. security

Security refers to all the measures that are taken to protect a place, or to ensure that only people with permission enter it or leave it.

4. boarding gate

Through boarding gate you can get on the plane.

5. international departure lobby

International passengers should go to international departure lobby for their leaving.

6. luggage check

An additional element that attached to your luggage which can save much more time for those with luggage to check or claim.

7. luggage claim area

A place to find your travelled luggage when you deplaned the flight.

8. conveyor

A conveyor or conveyor belt is a continuously moving strip of rubber or metal which is used in factories for moving objects along so that they can be dealt with as quickly as possible.

9. domestic transfer

The process you get off one flight and board the other nationwide.

2.1.1.2 Useful Sentence Patterns

Asking for Directions

Is this the right way to...?

Could you please show me the way to...?

Excuse me, where can I get to...?

How can I get there?

Which way is it?

Could you please tell me where the lavatory is?

Excuse me, I wonder if you could tell me how to get there.

Replies

Just over there.

In the corner.

On the second floor.

Turn left / right.

Go down this street and turn right at the second intersection. You'll find a tall building with the name of the hotel.

It's quite a distance from here. If you don't have a car, you'd better take a bus.

It's about a block down the street.

2.1.2　Dialogues

2.1.2.1　Where should we board the plane?

(C: Clerk　P: Passenger)

Setting: The passenger put his 2 pieces of luggage on the belt.

C: Next, please. Hello, Sir, your passport?

P: Hello, I am checking in for flight MU923 to San Francisco.

C: OK. Which seat do you prefer?

P: I'd like a window seat, non-smoking section.

C: One moment, please, let me check... Sir, your seat is 18A, non-smoking, window. Do you have any luggage to check in?

P: Yes, I have two.

C: Please put them on the belt.

P: Could you please tell me where we can board the plane?

C: After checking in, you should go through security, and your boarding gate is No. 52 on the second floor, international departure lobby.

P: Thank you.

C: My pleasure. Here is your ticket and passport, and here is your boarding pass and luggage check. Have a nice trip, goodbye, Sir.

2.1.2.2　How do I get to the luggage claim and domestic transfer?

(C: Clerk　P: Passenger)

Setting: Mr. Wang and his wife are inquiring about how to get to the Luggage Claim Area.

C: Sir, what can I do for you?

P1: We deplaned from flight CZ2564 just now. How do I get to the luggage claim area?

C: You may though this gate and you will see the luggage claim lobby. You can find your flight number on LED screen. Then you will see on which conveyor you can claim your luggage.

P1: Thank you very much.

Setting: Mr. Wang and his wife are inquiring about the connection formalities.

P2: Good morning, Miss. I've just arrived Chengdu and I'm going to fly to Guangzhou in the evening. Here is my ticket.

C: Yes, Sir. Your connecting flight is CA1297 from Chengdu to Guangzhou at 6:30 p.m.

P2: How can I make my connection?

C: You should check in at the Domestic Transfer Counter. It's on the second floor, north side.

P2: Should I have to claim and transfer my luggage?

C: Don't worry about your luggage, our ground staff will help them transfer to connecting flight.

P2: That's really very nice. Thank you very much.

C: Don't mention it. Please remember go to the check in counter for the connection procedure no later than 5:30 p.m.

2.1.3　Cultural Background

Boarding Pass

A boarding pass is a document provided by an airline during check-in, giving a passenger permission to board the airplane for a particular flight. As a minimum, it identifies the passenger. The flight number and the date ad scheduled time for departure. In some cases, flyers can check in online and print the boarding passes themselves.

Generally a passenger with an electronic ticket will only need a boarding pass. If a passenger has a paper airline ticket, that ticket may be required to be attached to the boarding pass for him or her to board the aircraft. The paper boarding pass (and ticket, if any), or portions, are sometimes collected and counted for cross-check of passenger counts by gate agents, but more frequently are scanned. The standards for bar codes and magnetic stripes on boarding passes are published by IATA. The bar code standard (BCBP) defines the 2D bar code printed on paper boarding passes or sent to mobile phones for electronic boarding passes. The magnetic stripe standard (ATB2) expired in 2010. For "connecting flights" there will be a boarding pass needed for each new flight regardless of whether a different aircraft is boarded.

Most airports and airlines have automatic readers that will verify the validity of the boarding pass at the jet way door or boarding gate. This also automatically updates the airline's database that shows the passenger has boarded and the seat is used, and that the checked baggage for that passage for that passenger may stay aboard. This speeds up the paperwork process at the gate, but requires passengers with papers with paper tickets to check in, surrender the ticket and receive the digitized boarding pass.

Whenever possible, attendants should help the passengers to find their assigned seats. The seat number is indicated on the boarding pass. It is special pass which shows that the passenger has completed the check-in process and can board this flight. It shows the flight number, the class (first or economy), and the seat assignment.

The seat number includes 2 parts, an Arabic numeral with an English letter, for example, 4C, 7B, 30D, etc. The numeral indicates which row the seat is in, and the English letter indicates which line it is in.

2.2　Information Inquiry

2.2.1　Language Points and Useful Sentence Patterns

2.2.1.1　Language Points

1. name list

A paper listed names, such as class names, passenger names, etc.

2. reservation card

A card tells your flight number or its change.

3. international passenger

Passengers who are travelling aboard served as an international passenger.

4. visa

A visa is an official document, or a stamp put in your passport, which allows you to enter or leave a particular country.

5. airport fee

Airport fee is used to repair or maintain the smooth use of the airport.

6. passport control

The international passengers need to be checked of the validity of their passport and control when entry or out of a country.

2.2.1.2　Useful Sentence Patterns

1. Inquiring One's Needs and Wants

Would you like fruit juice?

What / How about your preference?

Don't you like love music?

What do you think of a window seat?

Are you fond of taking the aisle seat?

2. Asking for Information

Can you tell me something about...?

Sorry to trouble you, but could you tell me the weather in Beijing...?

Do you by any chance know...?

I'd like to know more about your physical condition.

I'm afraid I'm not quite clear about...

I wonder if you could explain about...in more detail.

2.2.2 Dialogues

2.2.2.1 Could I try finding a person on the passengers' name list?

(C: Clerk   P: Passenger)

P: My friend is scheduled to come from New York on flight MU736 today. Could I try finding him on your passengers' name list?

C: Certainly. May I have his full name?

P: Yang Hua.

C: Just a second and I'll check. Sorry, there isn't a Yang Hua on the name list.

P: Is there anyway to check his actual flight?

C: Let me check his reservation card. It shows that he has changed his reservation to MU736 tomorrow. It leaves New York at 10:25 a.m. and arrives in Beijing at 4:40 p.m.

P: Really? He did not tell me about the change.

C: You can call again tomorrow afternoon. We'll tell if he is definitely taking that flight.

P: Thank you for your information.

C: You're welcome.

2.2.2.2 Is there any way I can do to get on the plane?

(C: Clerk   P: Passenger)

P: Good morning, Miss. This is my first time to fly by air. Is there anything I can do to get on the plane? I don't know the procedures before I get on board.

C: What is your destination, Sir?

P: Tokyo.

C: International passenger should get all your travel documents ready, such as your passport with visa, ticket, health card and make sure your reservation status is OK.

P: What does that mean?

C: That means you can get your seat on that flight, I'll check it for you, your passport, please?

P: Here it is. I'm afraid I just requested but not confirmed my seat.

C: Let me see, now it is OK, you seat number is 22K. Please go there and pay your airport fee first, and then go into the departure counter to check in for your flight, and check your luggage. After this, you'll get a boarding pass. Then you should follow other passengers to go through the passport control and the security check. When it's time to board the plane, you many board your flight.

P: Thanks a lot.

2.2.3 Cultural Background

Domestic and International Passengers

In most countries, the domestic passenger comes to the airport, presents his ticket at the airline counter, checks in his baggage, and boards his flight. Upon arrival at his destination, he picks up his baggage and goes on his way.

The international passenger, on the other hand, goes through a much more complicated process. For the departing passenger, there may be government regulations with which to comply in addition to the airline check-in process. Almost all countries have at least three formalities through which the passenger must pass. They include passport and visa control, health check, and customs inspection of the passenger's baggage. Not until the passenger has been cleared through all of these procedures is he legally free to enter the country to which he is traveling. Almost all countries also have forms of one sort or another that the international passenger must fill out. This is usually done on the plane before it lands. The most customary of these forms would be the disembarkation card.

2.3　Flight Delay

2.3.1　Language Points and Useful Sentence Patterns

2.3.1.1　Language Points

1. scheduled departure time

The departure time scheduled according to the ticket.

2. mechanical problem

A mechanical problem related to aeroplane is often something related to engine.

3. terminal building

The terminal building is a place for passengers to go through airport procedures, such as check in, security check, passport control, the Customs and quarantine inspection, etc.

4. thunderstorm

A thunderstorm is a storm in which there is thunder and lightning and a lot of heavy rain, and it has a severe effect on flights' taking off and landing.

5. air traffic control

Air traffic control is the activity of organizing the routes that aircraft should follow, and telling pilots by radio which routes they should take.

6. accommodation

Accommodation is used to refer to buildings or rooms where people live or stay.

7. ID card

Identification card is an official document for native people to verify their identity.

2.3.1.2　Useful Sentence Patterns

1. Making an Apology

I can't tell you how sorry I am.

Please accept my sincere apology.

I'm awfully sorry.

I'm sorry, but...

Sorry about the inconvenience.

My apologies.

2. Beginning an Explanation about Something

I'm sorry to say that our flight is delayed due to...

I'm sorry, but the plane has something wrong. The flight will be delayed.

Wait a minute. Let me explain. The reason...

This is a short flight. We only serve beverages and refreshments on board.

I don't mean that. What I meant was...

The fact of the matter is that...

Well, what happened was...

Give me chance to explain...

It's not true. The fact of the matter is...

2.3.2　Dialogues

2.3.2.1　The delay is due to some mechanical difficulties

(G: Ground Staff　P: Passenger)

P: Excuse me, Miss. My flight is 3U4122 to Qingdao at 11:10 a.m., but it's 15 minutes past the scheduled departure time.

G: Sorry, Sir, out flight is delayed due to some mechanical problems.

P: What happened with the flight?

G: Some problems with the engine, our flight engineers are making a careful examination of the plane.

P: It's awful! Will it be delayed even longer?

G: I'm sorry we haven't received any further information. But we'll keep you informed. You can pay attention to our airport announcement as well.

P: Well, I do hope the flight will take off soon.

2.3.2.2　How long will the delay last?

(G: Ground Staff　P: Passenger)

Announcement: Passengers for Qingdao, may I have your attention, please? Flight 3U4122 for Qingdao will be delayed for an hour. Please wait in the terminal building. We will announce again when we get further information. Thank you.

P: Miss! I was wondering why our plane hasn't taken off yet? We've been waiting here for almost one hour! I have an important meeting in Qingdao, if the flight does not depart soon, I'll Miss it!

G: Sorry, Sir, I understand. But the weather forecast says that there is a thunderstorm with hail in Qingdao right now.

P: How long will the delay last? May be it will be clear before we get there.

G: It says it won't stop raining in the future 2 hours. We can not take off under bad weather conditions.

P: OK. Safety should be put at the first place.

2.3.2.3　Who will pay me for the accommodation?

(G: Ground Staff　P: Passenger)

P: Good afternoon. I wonder if my flight has been delayed.

G: What is your flight number?

P: Flight CA738 to Moscow.

G: Yes, it has been delayed due to air traffic control.

P: How long will the delay last?

G: I'm sorry. It's not sure yet. Maybe several hours or maybe overnight.

P: Overnight? How could I arrange my accommodation?

G: Don't worry. If you have to stay here for the night, we will be responsible for your meals and accommodation. We really apologize for the inconvenience caused by this delay.

P: It seems that what I can do is to wait for your news. Thank you for telling me all.

G: Thank you for your understanding and cooperation.

2.3.2.4　Could you tell the reason why my Flight has been cancelled?

(G: Ground Staff　P: Passenger)

Announcement: Passengers for Qingdao, may I have your attention, please? Flight 3U4122 for Qingdao has been cancelled. Please go to counter E4 to change to the following flights of Air China. Sorry for the inconvenience caused.

P: Could you tell the reason why my flight has been cancelled?

C: Sorry, Miss. Flight CA6357 to Qingdao has been cancelled due to some mechanical problems.

P: But I plan to sign a contract with Donald & Co. tomorrow so I have to get there tonight.

C: Don't worry. I can rebook you on the following flights. There are 2 flights left for Qingdao today, 3:10 p.m. and 7:25 p.m., you can choose one of them depending on your schedule.

P: I'll take the 3:10 p.m one, I don't want to wait so long.

C: OK. Your ID card, please.

2.3.3 Cultural Background

Airports

Airports provide air transportation for people, freight, mail, perishable foods, and other important items. To achieve this, an airport is used for the landing and takeoff of aircraft. An airport is composed of several areas and buildings that are designed to serve the needs of both passengers and aircraft.

Runways are the long, narrow concrete areas where airplanes take off and land. Taxiways are concrete roads that aircraft follow from the runways to the terminal building. The terminal building also contains ticket and baggage counters. The control tower is located near the terminal building. From this tower, air traffic control coordinates aircraft movements both in the air and on the ground. For security purposes, access to major airports is usually limited to special roads. Many airports have large car parking areas on the ground or in multistory car parks.

Airports are among the busiest transportation centers in a region. The business they created is vital to the world economy and individual national economies. Airports are so important to a city that many companies will not locate factories or offices in cities that do not have an adequate airport. There are three major types of airports: military, general aviation, and the commercial airports. Airports differ in size and layout depending on their function and the types of aircraft and traffic that use them.

Military airports have one or two paved runways, generally 3,000 to 4,600 meters long, or 10,000 to 15,000 feet long. These airports are used only by military aircraft. General aviation airports cater for small civil aircraft and are smaller than commercial airports. They are often located in rural areas or in small towns. General aviation airports have one or two runways from 900 to 1,500 meters long, or 3,000 to 5,000 feet long. Commercial airports are used by airlines. These airports may be small or large. Small commercial airports have one or two runways from 1,800 to 2,400 meters long. Large commercial airport usually have pairs of parallel runways from 3,000 to 3,700 meters in length.

2.4   Shopping at the Airport

2.4.1   Language Points and Useful Sentence Patterns

2.4.1.1   Language Points

1. purified plant

A product always some cosmetics made only from plant or only used plant extracts.

2. nutritious

Nutritious cosmetic contains substances which help you skin to be healthy or water-oil balanced.

3. duty-free

Duty free goods are sold at airports or on planes or ships at a cheaper price than usual because you do not have to pay import tax on them.

4. lotion

A lotion is a liquid that you use to clean, improve, or protect your skin or hair.

5. dispensable

If someone or something is dispensable they are not really needed.

6. additional

Additional things are extra things apart from the ones already present.

7. special offer

A special offer is a product, service, or program that is offered at reduced prices or rates.

8. declaration

A declaration is an official announcement or statement.

2.4.1.2   Useful Sentence Patterns

1. Money transactions

The perfume costs 41 dollars.

The scarves are 72 dollars each.

Forty-one plus 72 makes 113 dollars.

Four times eight equals 32 dollars.

A hundred dollars minus 85 that's 15 dollars change.

That comes to 120 Euros.

How will you be paying? By card or with cash?

How would you like to pay?

Here's your receipt, your card and your gifts.

2. Making a recommendation

I suggest (that) you have your coats ready.

I suggest (that) you take the airport bus.

I suggest (that) you don't get up immediately.

Shall we go there and look for the vacant seat?

How about having an apple?

Don't you think it might be a good idea?

Wouldn't you like to try this one?

Why don't you...?

2.4.2　Dialogues

2.4.2.1　You can get the lowest price in the duty-free shop

(A: Attendant　P: Passenger)

A: Good morning, Madam. May I help you?

P: Ah, yea, I am looking for some cosmetics for my friends. Do you have any suggestions?

A: My pleasure. The CLARINS Shaping Facial Lift Total V contouring serum is quite popular. What is her skin type? Dry, oil or mix?

P: I have no idea. But I think she likes purified plant.

A: CLARINS is a French brand using plant extracts only.

P: Sounds good. I heard the Estee Lauder Advanced Night Repair was famous. How about it?

A: It is nutritious for middle-aged ladies. Now we have a sets of this product, including one 50ml Estee Lander Advanced Night Repair and one 15ml Estee Lander Advanced Night Repair Eye. The price is 920 RMB.

P: That's much cheaper than cosmetics counters.

A: Yes, you can get the lowest price in duty-free shops.

P: Do you have a yellow lotion, I can't name it, but I think it's a Clinique product.

A: Maybe it's Clinique 3-step skin care, the most famous one is Clinique Dramatically Different Moisturizing Gel or Lotion. Gel is for oil skin and Lotion is for dry and mix skin.

P: Can I only take one Lotion? I don't think I need 3-steps.

A: Sure, others may be dispensable for you.

P: OK. I need 3 sets Estee Lander and 3 Clinique Moisturizing Lotion, please wrap it up for me.

2.4.2.2　You cannot buy it at any other airports

(A: Attendant　P: Passenger)

P: Miss, I saw your "Hot Sale" sign on the window. Are there any additional discount?

A: Some are. Which brand are you looking for?

P: Coach bags.

A: This way please, here are discounted ones, Coach Swagger 21, Coach Mercer, Coach Dinky. We are offering a 20% additional discount on these discounted bags, really a super deal.

P: How much is Coach Swagger 21?

A: The original price is $754, 40% off is $452, with additional 20% off it comes down to $361. Under half! You cannot buy it at any other airports. It is a special offer only at our airport.

P: Sounds attractive. Can I have a try?

A: Sure. Here it is.

P: Not bad. It is my cup of tea. But I was thinking of changing a different style. Let me look around before I decide.

A: OK. If you have any questions please let me know. I am Cindy.

P: Thank you!

2.4.2.3   I want to buy a bottle of perfume

(A: Attendant   P: Passenger)

A: Morning, Sir, do you need some help?

P: I want to buy a bottle of perfume for my girlfriend. Do you have some recommendation?

A: Chanel No. 5, Dior J'adore, Lancome Miracle and Marc Jacobs Daisy are popular. You can have a look at them.

P: Oh, they are so amazing. I have no idea which one is the best. Maybe I can have all of these.

A: That will be the best choice because you have not to pay any duties on them.

P: I know. This is duty-free shop.

A: Yes, or else you need to pay the duty if you have got two bottles of perfume listed in your declaration form.

P: Even if it charges me some duty, I guess it's still cheaper than buying it locally, let alone no duties. I'll take them.

A: OK. Wait a moment.

2.4.3   Cultural Background

Duty-free Shops

Duty-free shops are retail outlets that are exempt from the payment of certain local or national taxes and duties, on the requirement that the goods sold will be sold to travelers who will take them out of the country. However, some countries impose duty on goods brought into the country, though they had been bought duty-free in another country, or when the value or quantity of such goods exceed an allowed limit.

Duty-free shops are often found in the international zone of international airports and sea ports, but goods can be also bought duty-free on board airplanes and passenger ships. Some countries have inwards duty free facilities, where arriving passengers can purchase duty free items immediately before going through customs. This not only saves the inconvenience of having to carry these items around the world but also solves the security problem mentioned above. Other countries such as Canada and Sweden have been considering duty free on arrival. The European Union does not permit arrivals duty free shopping, some EU airports sell goods on arrival in the baggage claim area described as "Tax-free", but these goods are all tax-paid sales, the local sales tax is discounted.

Goods sold to passengers on board ships or aircraft are tax free. The passenger can either consume them on board, or import them tax-free into the country they are traveling to, so long as they are within the traveler's duty-free allowance. Most tax regimes also allow travelers entering a country to bring in a certain amount of goods for personal use without paying tax on them, the so-called "duty-free allowance".

The goods purchased at duty-free shops at an airport must be exported intact (they cannot be consumed in the airport), and they are imported into the destination country under that country's own tax rules. In some countries, in order to ensure that goods are exported intact, they are hand-delivered in a closed bag to the passenger at the gate after his ticket is scanned.

2.5 Eating at the Airport

2.5.1 Language Points and Useful Sentence Patterns

2.5.1.1 Language Points

1. chain store

A chain store is one of several similar shops that are owned by the same person or company, especially one that sells a variety of things.

2. flavor

The taste of a dish, ice-cream, or other things.

3. voucher

A voucher is a ticket or piece of paper that can be used instead of money to pay for something.

4. cuisine

The cuisine of a country or district is the style of cooking that is characteristic of that place.

5. sliced chili sauce

A famous typical Sichuan cuisine, beef and ox tripe in chili sauce.

6. fish flavored pork

Stir fried pork with carrots, agarics, and caraway in chili sauce.

7. double-fried pork

Double cooked pork slices stir fried boiled pork slices with hot sauce twice cooked pork slices with hot sauce.

2.5.1.2 Useful Sentence Patterns

1. Asking If Somebody Agrees or Approves

Do you go along with me?

Do agree with me on this point?

Is it OK now?

Don't you feel it will work?

Would you concur with such a proposal?

Would you agree with what I said just now?

Does that meet your need?

Have I got it right?

Replics

I quite agree with you.

That's my opinion, too.

I suppose so.

You've got something there.

I'm afraid I have a different opinion.

I really don't approve your behavior.

2. Let Other People Make the Decision

I'll leave it up to you.

I'd be happy to do whatever you think best.

It doesn't matter to me whether...

It's entirely at your decision.

I think it all depends on how you feel about it.

You can make the decision.

2.5.2 Dialogues

2.5.2.1 Welcome to Subway

(C: Clerk   P: Passenger)

C: Welcome to Subway, how may I help you?

P: This is my first time to China, to my surprise, you have Subway in China.

C: Yes, Sir. It has many chain stores all over China, like KFC and McDonald.

P: Is the flavor the same as American.

C: Sure, we use imported chicken breast, beef, ham, tuna and ingredients.

P: OK. Give me one tuna sandwich, one honey oat, two sweet pies, a salad and a cup of hot milk tea.

C: Wait a moment…87 RMB, Sir.

P: I download some food voucher on you website, can I use it?

C: Of course. Plus the 10 RMB voucher, you need to pay 77 RMB.

P: Thank you, here is the money.

2.5.2.2　Are you ready to order?

(C: Clerk　P: Passenger)

C: Welcome, Sir, here is our menu, are you ready to order?

P: I felt difficult to read it because I only recognize a few words. What is your special cuisine? Do you have some recommendation?

C: Do you mind trying some spicy food?

P: That's OK. We want to try some different Chinese food. I heard that Chinese food is divided into 8 most famous cuisines.

C: Yes, it has Shandong cuisine, Guangdong cuisine, Hunan cuisine, Huizhou cuisine, etc. Our restaurant mainly sells Sichuan cuisine which is made up of spicy and hot food.

P: Sounds interesting. Is Mapo Tofu on your menu?

C: Sure, it is a typical Sichuan dish. Our specialty also includes: boiled fish, sliced chili sauce, spicy chicken, fish flavored pork, and double-fried pork.

P: Oh, I guess boiled fish tastes lighter than others.

C: No, maybe you misunderstood "boiled", it doesn't mean using water to boil, actually we use hot chili oil pour down on fresh fish filet.

P: Really? Hot oil can cook the fish? I will try this.

C: Anything else?

P: Mapo Tofu, sliced chili sauce and Sichuan noodles with peppery sauce, please.

2.5.3　Cultural Background

Food and Culture

The main difference between Chinese and Western eating habits is that unlike the West, where everyone has their own plate of food, in China the dishes are placed on the table and everybody shares.

To the Chinese, food is life but it is also health and a symbol of other good things such as luck and prosperity. Chinese are very proud of their culture of cuisine and do their best to show their hospitality. Sometimes the Chinese host uses his chopsticks to put food in a guest's bowl or plate. This is a sigh of politeness. The appropriate thing to do would be to eat whatever it is and say how tasty it is. But Westerners always feel uncomfortable with this, so a simple thank-you and leaving the food there may be the best reaction.

For both Chinese and Westerners, table manners are considered essential and the distinctive courtesies displayed will invariably add to the enjoyment of people's meals.

Some behavior at the table is considered impolite in Chinese culture. For example, people can't stick their chopsticks upright in their rice bowl, the spout of the teapot can't face anyone, and people can't tap on their bowl with their chopsticks.

As for Westerners, they have their own table manners. In Britain, even today, people are judged by their table manners, especially when eating out or attending formal functions. When dining, people can't pick up the soup bowl and drink from it. If one wants a particular dish on the other side of the table, they will ask someone to pass the dish instead of reaching across the table for it himself. People don't put bones on the table. They leave them on their plate. They don't talk or laugh with food in their mouth. They don't clean their face with their napkin. It is for people to put on their lap. The point of eating out at a nice restaurant is to have a good time and enjoy a good meal. If they're happy and satisfied, leaving a generous tip (usually 15%- 20% of the bill) is considered polite.

2.6　Foreign Exchange

2.6.1　Language Points and Useful Sentence Patterns

2.6.1.1　Language Points

1. currency

The money used in a particular country is referred to as its currency.

2. exchange rate

The exchange rate of a country's unit of currency is the amount of another country's currency that you get in exchange for it.

3. signature

Your signature is your name, written in your own characteristic way, often at the end of a document to indicate that you wrote the document or that you agree with what it says.

4. draft

A draft is an early version of a letter, book, or speech.

5. L / C

Short term of letter of credit. A letter of credit is a letter written by a bank authorizing another bank to pay someone a sum of money. Letters of credit are often used by importers and exporters.

6. light rail

A continental transportation using solar and wind-powered electric to transit and freight.

7. freight

Freight is goods that are transported by lorries, trains, ships, or airplanes.

2.6.1.2 Useful Sentence Patterns

1. Expressing Ability

I'm sure I'm able to do the work.

I'm capable of...

I'm certain I'd be able to...

I would say I was capable.

I can make it.

I can handle this.

Let me solve it.

2. Expressing Inability

I think it's beyond me.

I am not sure I can handle this.

I can't do it.

I can't manage to open that door.

I'm not good at it.

She has no idea to run a company.

Lily has no experience.

3. Inquiring about Satisfaction

How do you like this one?

Are you satisfied with it?

How are you enjoying...?

What do you think of...?

It is what you want?

Will it do?

Replies

That's great!

It's just what I was looking for.

I'm quite satisfied with it.

It's too exaggerated.

I really thought it would be more perfect.

2.6.2 Dialogues

2.6.2.1 Could you change some money for me?

(C: Clerk   P: Passenger)

C: Good evening, Sir. How may I help you?

P: Good evening, could you change some money for me?

C: OK. What kind of foreign currency have you got?

P: European Dollars.

C: Today's exchange rate is 7.536 RMB to 1 European Dollar. How much do you plan to change?

P: One thousand European Dollars.

C: Could you please show me your passport?

P: Here you are.

C: Please fill in the Exchange Foreign Currency Form and sign you name in the bottom "Signature Column".

P: OK...Is that all right?

C: That's right. Here is the money, 7,536 RMB, please check it.

P: Thank you very much.

2.6.2.2　May I see the L / C and your passport, please?

(C: Clerk　P: Passenger)

P: Is here currency exchange service counter?

C: Yes, Sir. What kind of service do you need?

P: I want to exchange my draft.

C: May I see the L / C and your passport, please?

P: Sure, here you are.

C: What kind of currency do you want to exchange?

P: Some RMB, some dollars, please. What is the rate?

C: We exchange your draft at a different rate from notes. Today's rate for US dollar is 6.1:1. Please fill in this form and sign here.

P: OK. By the way, where is the light rail station to downtown?

C: You may go outside the terminal building, on the opposite bank of freight center, under a big green board. Here is your passport and cash, have a nice day.

P: Thank you.

2.6.3　Cultural Background

The Responsibilities of Flight Attendant's Before Take-off

When passengers begin to board the plane, flight attendants will stand at cabin doors to welcome passengers warmly. You will greet passengers with smiles and lead them to their seats, especially for those who are old, weak, sick, disabled and young. If passengers are blocking the aisles, and you should remind them politely. You help passengers place their baggage. The space of overhead bins should be properly arranged. If the passenger's hand baggage is not in accordance with the safety regulation; you have to notify the chief purser / purser. If necessary, the baggage has to be checked. When everybody is on board, you also count the numbers of passengers.

Before taking off, flight attendants should introduce emergency equipment by broadcasting and conduct certain safety checks. For example, you have to confirm the qualification of passengers sitting next to the emergency exits, check whether the items in the overhead bins are properly arranged and lock the overhead bins.

While taxiing, the announcers make announcements to greet passengers and play the safety demonstration video. You will also dim the cabin lights, conduct safety inspection again and then make safety report to the purser or chief purser.

In the following is a safety check list.

1. Each passenger has his seat belt fastened.

2. Tray tables are closed.

3. Seat backs are in upright position.

4. Carry-on items are securely stowed and the stowage bins are locked.

5. The dining cars are fixed and the power switches of oven and teakettle are off.

6. No smoking in the cabin.

7. Lavatories are suspended.

Unit 3
Arranging Check-in

3.1 Declaration

3.1.1 Language Points and Useful Sentence Patterns

3.1.1.1 Language Points

1. for business

People travel to some place for business affairs.

2. boarding pass

A pass allows passenger to board a ship or plane.

3. declare

People who take international flight should make a declaration (of dutiable goods) to a customs official.

4. go through security

Everyone who travels by air must go through airport security checkpoint, which makes sure that any dangerous articles can't be taking aboard the airplane.

5. belt

A moving belt that transports objects from place to place.

6. Li-ion battery

A portable battery is made of lithium, which is easy to explode as the pressure in the cabin changes. According to the CAAC's regulation, Li-ion battery can't be taken into the passengers' cabin.

3.1.1.2 Useful Sentence Patterns

1. Showing Directions and Positions

It's just to your right.

It's on the 2nd floor.

It's next to...

It's located in/at...

It's over there.

It's just around the corner.

2. Expressing Certainty and Uncertainty

Certainly

I am sure that...

It's certain that...

I can say for certain that...

Of course!

Uncertainty

I'm not sure that...

It's uncertain that / what / whether...

It's hard to say...

It all depends.

3. Expressing Disappointment

What a shame!

What a pity!

How disappointed I was!

I'm feeling so depressed.

I'm feeling down.

3.1.2   Dialogues

3.1.2.1   What's the purpose of your visit?

(C: Clerk   P: Passenger)

C: Good morning, Sir.

P: Good morning.

C: May I have your ticket and passport, please?

P: Sure. Here is my ticket and passport.

C: What's the purpose of your visit?

P: I travel to Hanover for business.

C: Great. Here is your passport and your boarding pass, please. Have a nice trip.

P: Thanks a lot.

C: You're welcome.

3.1.2.2   Do you have anything to declare?

(C: Clerk   P: Passenger)

C: Would you give me your ticket and passport, please?

P: Here you are.

C: Have you got anything to declare?

P: What should be declared actually?

C: You must declare all the things listed on the declaration form. Also you need to declare the things that are not for your own use.

P: No, I think. I just bring some gifts for my friends in the suitcase. And a laptop is for my personal use.

C: That's all right. You can go through security now. Have a nice trip.

3.1.2.3   Would you please open your case?

(C: Clerk   P: Passenger)

C: Excuse me, Sir. Would you please put your case on the belt?

P: Yes, Sir.

C: What's inside your suitcase? Would you please open it?

P: No problem.

C: Sorry, Sir. According to the safety regulation, Li-ion battery are not allowed to be taken in the checked baggage.

P: I'm sorry, I don't know the regulation. What shall I do with it now?

C: You can take it in your carry-on handbag.

P: Oh, that's great. I'm afraid I have to get rid of it. Thank you very much.

C: You're welcome.

3.1.2.4   Could you show me the article you want to declare?

(C: Clerk   P: Passenger)

P: Shall I go through the customs now?

C: Yes. You need to fill in the declaration forms.

P: All right.

C: Do you have anything to declare?

P: I have got some Chinese-made cigarettes for my friends.

C: Could you show me the article you want to declare, please?

P: Sure. Here they are.

C: Oh, there are 4 packets of cigarettes. These exceed the allowance of free. I'm afraid you have to be charged some duty on them.

P: How much do I have to pay for them? And where should I go?

C: You just go straight along the main passage. The customs counter is just to your right.

P: Thank you for your help.

C: It's my pleasure.

3.1.3   Cultural Background

China Customs Declaration

The followings need to be declared according to the China Customs Luggage Declaration Form when entering into China:

1. Any item that will be left in China whose value exceeds 2,000 CNY.

2. More than 400 cigarettes or 100 cigars and 1.5 liters of alcoholic beverages (alcohol measure above 12 degrees).

3. Foreign currency greater than 5,000 US dollars or the equivalent, or 20,000 CNY.

4. Animals and animal products, microorganism, biological products, human tissue, blood

and blood products.

5. Transceiver, communications devices.

6. Any items prohibited and limited according to the laws of the People's Republic of China.

7. Luggage needs to be transported separately.

8. Cargo, commercial samples, advertising items.

The followings need to be declared according to the China Customs Luggage Declaration Form when exiting the country:

1. Foreign currency above 5,000 US dollars or equivalent, or 20,000 CNY.

2. Gold, silver and other valuable items.

3. Cultural relics, endangered animals and plants as well as their products, biological species resources.

4. Transceiver, communication devices.

5. Any items prohibited and limited according to the laws of the People's Republic of China.

6. Cargo, commercial sample, advertising items.

3.2 Boarding Pass

3.2.1 Language Points and Useful Sentence Patterns

3.2.1.1 Language Points

1. seat preference

Passenger can choose the seat they like better.

2. vegetarian meal

Meals are provided for special passengers who are vegetarian. There are some different kinds of vegetarians. The vegan or total vegetarian diet includes only foods from plants: fruits, vegetables, grains, seeds, and nuts. The lacto-over-vegetarian diet includes plant foods plus cheese and other dairy products.

3. standby passenger

A passenger needs to refund ticket.

4. overbooking

Airlines sell more tickets than are available.

5. departure time

The time, at which a plane is scheduled to depart from a given point of origin.

6. upgrading

Assign to a higher class, such as business class or first class.

7. international and domestic flights

International flights are flights taking off in one country and landing in another.

Domestic flights begin and end in the same country.

3.2.1.2 Useful Sentence Patterns

1. Expressing Preference

I prefer... rather than...

I like... better than...

Something is my first priority.

2. Expressing Happiness and Unhappiness

Happiness

That's prefect.

It's a wonderful idea.

That's good to hear.

I'm so glad to...

Unhappiness

Oh, my God. That's so bad.

It's awful.

I can't stand...

I can't bear...

How ridiculous it was!

3. Expressing Complaints

I have never seen such silly things before.

I am ashamed of you.

You shouldn't be so careless.

Sorry. I don't appreciate the way you speak to me.

3.2.2 Dialogues

3.2.2.1 May I have a seat preference, please?

(C: Clerk   P: Passenger)

C: Good morning, Sir. Please show me your ticket and passport.

P: Wait a moment, please. Here you are.

C: Thanks.

P: May I have a seat preference, please?

C: Of course.

P: I prefer a seat in the front of the cabin, a window seat is better.

C: Let me check in the computer. Please wait a moment. Yes. We still have a few vacant seats.

P: Great. It's very kind of you.

C: Here is your passport and boarding pass, please.

P: All right. Thank you again.

3.2.2.2   Can I have a vegetarian meal?

(C: Clerk   P: Passenger)

P: Excuse me, Miss. I can't eat any of the food on this menu. I'm a vegetarian. Do you have a vegetarian meal?

C: I'm sorry, Sir. We can offer you a vegetarian meal. I will check in the galley. Please wait for a while.

P: Great. What's the main course?

C: We have spiced vegetable stew with rice, fried noodles with vegetables and marinated vegetables. What would you prefer?

P: I'd like to have spiced vegetable stew with rice. By the way, what else do you have?

C: We also have vegetable hors d'oeuvre, vegetable soup and fruit salad.

P: Vegetable soup and fruit salad, please.

C: Sure. Here you are. Enjoy your meal.

P: Thanks a lot.

3.2.2.3   I am a standby passenger on that flight

(C: Clerk   P: Passenger)

C: Good afternoon, Miss.

P: Good afternoon. Can you help me to arrange check-in again?

C: What's wrong with your flight?

P: I am a standby passenger on the prior flight. When I checked in, I was just informed that there were no more seats on that flight. Why did that happen?

C: First of all, I should say sorry to you. Generally, airline companies sell more seats than they actually have in order to avoid loss. Once all passengers check in, there must be someone who can't board. But we can assist you to change flight.

P: What? How ridiculous it was. I will have an important meeting tomorrow. I must fly today.

C: I apologize for any inconvenience that we caused. If anyone can't be boarding due to overbooking, they can change flight or refund tickets.

P: Can you help me to change the earliest flight? I must leave today.

C: Of course. I arrange the earliest flight for you right now. Please wait for a moment.

P: That's good to hear that.

C: Miss, here is your passport and boarding pass, please. Your new departure time is 7:30 p.m. Please be boarding at gate 20.

P: Okay, goodbye.

C: Bye.

3.2.2.4 Do you mind upgrading your ticket to the first class?

(C: Clerk   P: Passenger)

C: Next, please.

P: Good afternoon.

C: Good afternoon, Sir. May I see your ticket and passport, please?

P: Yes, here you are.

C: Okay. Sorry, Sir. I'm sorry to tell you that there is no seat in the economy class.

P: Oh, my God. What's wrong with your company? I bought the ticket half months ago.

C: Every company would sell more tickets than they have seats on the international and domestic flights.

P: So it means I can't board today?

C: No, it doesn't. I just checked the system. There is a seat available in the first class. Do you mind upgrading your ticket to the first class?

P: Okay. But do I have to pay for the price difference?

C: No, our company will pay for it.

P: It seems there is no better choice than that.

C: Thank you for your understanding.

3.2.3 Cultural Background

Basic Responsibilities as a Flight Attendant

The most visible aspects of a flight attendant's job may be safety demonstrations and serving refreshments to passengers, but the position actually carries a considerable amount of responsibility. A flight attendant acts as an ambassador between the airline and its customers by making passengers feel comfortable during the flight. Flight attendants are also effectively the administrative staff on board the aircraft, responsible for the reporting and inventory work that keeps a flight running smoothly. Their most important duty, however, is seeing to the safety of everyone on board.

Passenger Comfort

To better impart a pleasant flying experience, flight attendants spend much of their in-flight time seeing to the comfort and needs of passengers. Pre-flight, flight attendants ease frustration and wait time by helping passengers to their seats and assisting with the stowing of carry-on luggage. They see to passengers' comfort by distributing sleep masks or blankets, and some airlines provide headsets or magazines if requested. Depending on the flight length, flight attendants may serve beverages and food as many as three times to passengers and to cockpit crews. Throughout the flight, flight attendants respond to passenger requests and fulfill them as much as possible. At the end of the flight, the attendants help passengers with their carry-on luggage and exiting the plane. These duties keep an attendant busy, but they also help build a relationship between passengers and the airline.

Administrative Duties

The less visible responsibilities of a flight attendant are nonetheless vital to the daily functions of airline flights. They must attend flight briefings to be apprised of any special passenger considerations and what to expect in-flight; no flight is exactly the same. Once on board, the attendant takes inventory of refreshments and first aid equipment and alerts appropriate personnel in case of shortages. During flight, it is the flight attendant's responsibility to keep track of money earned from purchased beverages or headset use and record the sales. At the end of the flight, attendants submit reports to the airline with flight details, including any medical issues encountered and the cabin's condition.

Passenger Safety

The first priority for flight attendants is seeing to the safety of every passenger on board. They are the ones providing safety demonstrations or setting up a video with safety directions to inform passengers of how to use the lifesaving devices aboard the plane. Attendants are responsible for securing the aircraft's doors and making sure emergency equipment and exits are functioning properly. Attendants secure any loose items around the cabin and check passengers for correct observance of safety procedures to prevent hazards mid-flight. Should any passenger engage in unsafe behavior during the flight, attendants respond by informing the passenger of the infraction and enforcing safety procedures if necessary?

Emergencies

In emergencies, flight attendants take the lead in aiding passengers. This may be as simple as providing reassurance during episodes of turbulence or as serious as administering first aid or evacuating passengers from the plane. Flight attendants must be prepared to provide direction and instruction for emergency landings and to assist passengers out of emergency exits and with emergency equipment. Should a medical emergency occur during flight, an attendant assesses the condition of the passenger, performs first aid if needed and, upon landing, informs the cockpit crew of the situation? The flight attendants also report any malfunctions encountered so they may be tended to after landing.

3.3   Baggage Check

3.3.1   Language Points and Useful Sentence Patterns

3.3.1.1   Language Points

1. baggage check

A type of check designed for the checked baggage.

2. weight allowance

Weight limit set by airline companies. If passengers' luggage is overweight, they have to take the extra items out of their luggage or pay excess baggage.

3. connecting flight

A flight with an intermediate stop and a change of aircraft (possibly a change of airlines).

3.3.1.2　Useful Sentence Patterns

1. Asking for The Destination

Where are you flying today?

What is your destination?

Where are you planning to fly today?

2. Expressing Appreciation

Thank you very much.

Thanks a lot.

Thank you for your carefulness.

Thank you for your understanding.

I sincerely appreciated your help.

3. Expressing Wishes

Have a nice trip.

I wish you have a fine trip.

I hope you have a pleasant journey.

3.3.2　Dialogues

3.3.2.1　How many pieces of luggage do you have?

(C: Clerk　P: Passenger)

C: Good morning, Sir. May I have your ticket and passport, please?

P: Here you are.

C: Thank you. Do you have any luggage to check in?

P: Yes. It's here.

C: How many pieces of luggage do you have?

P: Just a suitcase.

C: That's okay. Please put it on the conveyor belt. Here is your boarding pass and passport. And your baggage check is stuck on the back of your ticket.

P: Thank you very much.

C: You're welcome. Have a nice trip.

3.3.2.2　Is it overweight?

(C: Clerk　P: Passenger)

C: Good morning, Miss. Could you show me your ticket and passport, please?

P: Okay, here you are.

C: Do you have any luggage to check in?

P: Yes, I do. I have a suitcase to check in, here.

C: Okay, please put it on the belt.

P: Sure.

C: I'm afraid, Miss. Your luggage is over the weight allowance.

P: Oh, what should I do if it is overweight?

C: You take the international flight. According to the regulations, the weight allowance is 20 kilos. Your suitcase is 26 kilos, so it's 6 kilos heavier than that of the regulations. You have to pay for the excess kilos.

P: How much do I have to pay?

C: You need to check it in at the overweight luggage counter next to the Inquire Desk.

P: Okay. Thanks a lot.

C: You're welcome.

3.3.2.3   Is there anything needing special treatment?

(C: Clerk   P: Passenger)

C: Good afternoon, Sir.

P: Good afternoon.

C: Where are you flying today?

P: I' m flying to San Francisco.

C: May I see your ticket and passport, please?

P: Sure. Here it is.

C: Okay, thank you. Do you have any luggage to check in?

P: Yes, I have only one box to check in.

C: Please put it on the belt. By the way, is there anything to be treated specially?

P: Ah, there is a china tea set in this box.

C: Okay, I stick an "extra care" label on the box. That will be sound for long-haul flight.

P: Thank you for your carefulness.

C: It's my pleasure.

3.3.2.4   You can check-in your baggage all the way through to your destination

(C: Clerk   P: Passenger)

C: Next, please.

P: Good morning, Miss.

C: Good morning. Where are you flying today?

P: I'm flying to Melbourne via Singapore.

C: May I have your ticket and passport, please?

P: Here you are.

C: Thank you. You got a connecting flight from Guangzhou to Melbourne via Singapore. Here are your two boarding passes and passport, please.

P: Thank you. What about my luggage? Do I have to check it out at Singapore airport and check it in again for the second section of flight?

C: No, you can check in your baggage all the way through to your destination.

P: Oh, that will be excellent. Thank you again.

C: That's all right. Have a nice trip.

3.3.3 Cultural Background

Top 10 Baggage Claim Tips

If you have to check luggage, you will have to pick it up in the baggage claim area, sometimes called the baggage reclaim area in some airports outside the U.S. No matter where you are in the world, you face the same kind of problems like the airline losing or damaging your bag or someone stealing your luggage. If you follow the tips below, you can avoid most baggage claim problems.

1. Try to pack less

The easiest way to avoid baggage claim problems is to not have any checked bags. If you plan on checking two bags, and you find that you can travel with only one checked bag, than do so. If you can get by with just a carry-on bag, that would be an even better idea. In the U.S., most airlines allow you take one carry on bag, and one smaller item that can be placed under your seat. Also, there are many exceptions to carry on limits for things like baby strollers, medical devices, and child seats.

2. Make your bag easy to find

Many bags look alike, so do something to make it easy to find your bag quickly, like tying a bright ribbon to a handle or placing a decal on the side of your bag. If you have more than one bag, they may not be next to each other on the baggage carousel, so it is very important that each one of your bags have some kind of unique identifying features.

3. Put your contact information on your bags and inside each bag

Many bags come with a tag with a little address card. Put your name and contact information. If you put an address, put one where you want the bag to be delivered. You many want to also put a phone number or email address where you can be reached when you are traveling. You may want to put the same information inside the bag as well.

4. Check the Information on the luggage tag

At the check in counter, when the airline puts their luggage tag on the bag, make sure that the information is correct. The most important information is the origin and destination airports, which are three-letter codes that will be in capital letters. If you don't know what they are for your departure and arrival airport, ask when you check in. Many tags will also have information about the flight number, and perhaps your name. Make sure that any identification number or other information on your bag's tag matches the information on your claim ticket.

5. Get to the baggage claim area before your bags do

After your plane gets to the gate, make your way to the baggage claim area. If you are in an unfamiliar airport with a large baggage claim area, there may be many baggage carousels. If you are not sure where to go, ask one of your airline's agents, or look for a baggage carousel board that lists which carousel will have your flight's bags. Even if you are the last person out of a crowded plane, you should be able to get to the baggage claim area ahead of your bags.

6. Get into position to grab your bag

By the time the baggage carousel starts and bags start to come out, there will likely be a crowd of people looking for bags. Because the baggage claim area is not in the secure part of the terminal, you may have to deal with many other people besides the passengers on your flight, including potential thieves. Don't be shy, and get close to the carousel so you grab your bag the first time it comes by.

7. Keep off the baggage carousel

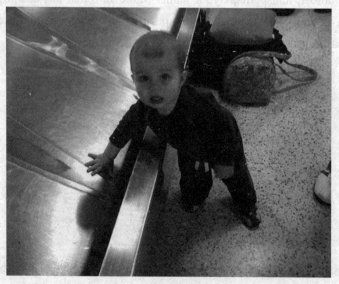

If you get to the carousel before the bags arrive, it may not be moving, and it may be tempting to either sit or rest on the carousel or to let your child play on it. Don't do it. The machine can start at any time and without warning. The last thing you need to let a simple bag pick up turn into a medical emergency.

8. Check your tags before you leave the baggage claim area

After you collect all your bags, check the tags on your bags with your claim ticket. The information should match. If they don't check your bag more closely to make sure you picked up the wrong bag. If you did, put it back on the carousel. If you accidentally take someone else's bag away from the baggage claim area, you will be responsible for returning it either to the airline or the bag's owner. Also, check to see that the number of bags you have matches the number of claim tickets you have. At the end of a long flight, you may be tired and not thinking clearly, so count your bags before you go.

9. Prepare for a missing, damaged, or stolen bag

Sometimes bad things happen to your checked luggage even if you take reasonable precautions. A little bit of preparation can make finding a lost or stolen bag or getting compensation for a lost or damaged bag much easier. A few things that you can do, including keeping receipts from when you purchased your bag or the items in the bag, taking pictures of the bag or its contents, and either remembering or writing down details like the color and size of the bag, the brand name, and anything that would help identify your bag.

10. Check your bag for damage before you leave

While airlines won't compensate you for broken wheels, minor scratches, missing handles, or other things that they consider to be normal wear and tear, if you have major damage to your bag that you think was caused by the airline, report it to the airline as soon as possible. It is best to do it before you leave the airport. If you file a claim, make sure that you follow the airline's procedures for making claim for lost or damaged luggage. You should also keep copies of any complaints you submit.

3.4　Security Check

3.4.1　Language Points and Useful Sentence Patterns

3.4.1.1　Language Points

1. security check

Security check includes frontier inspection, customs, health and quarantine, animal and plant quarantine and safety checks, and so on. One of the entry-exit personnel should carry out the procedures, it is important to ensure passenger safety precautions.

2. personal search

Security personnel in accordance with the regulations check passengers for dangerous goods or prohibited products with metal detectors and security gate.

3. special passage

A passage is special for VIPs, disabled passengers, or passengers with babies.

4. carry-on baggage

The baggage can be taken on board.

3.4.1.2　Useful Sentence Patterns

1. Offering Help

Can I help you?

How can I help you?

What can I do for you?

May I help you?

2. Saying Goodbye

Goodbye!

See you later.

Hope to see you again.

Look forward to seeing you again soon.

3.4.2　Dialogues

3.4.2.1　How should we go through the security check?

(C: Clerk　P: Passenger)

C: Hello, Sir. You have already been checked in. Here is your boarding pass and passport. Your boarding gate is No. 15. And your boarding time is 9:30 a.m. Now you should go to the security check.

P: Okay, thank you very much. But how should we go through the security check? And where should we go?

C: There is a check point in both A and B zone. Now you should take your carry-on baggage and go there for security check. The securer staff will tell you how you should do.

P: Great, thanks a lot.

C: You are welcome.

Setting: The man is going to the security check in A zone.

C: Morning, Sir. Please show your boarding pass and passport.

P: Sure. Here you are.

C: All right.

3.4.2.2　Does everyone have to receive a personal search?

(C: Clerk　P: Passenger)

P: Excuse me, Sir. Dose everyone has to receive a personal search?

C: Yes. According to the Civil Aviation Safety Regulation, everyone must receive the personal search. Anyone who refuses to accept the security check is not allowed to be boarding.

P: I was just wondering if the equipment is harmful for people's health.

S: Sir, passengers and their baggage will go through different channels. The former will go through this metal detector gate, which is no radiation for people. The later will be checked by the X-ray equipment, which is no harmful for people's baggage and even for films. There are two lead plates at each side of the X-ray equipment in order to keep the passengers and staffs away from the radiation.

P: Okay, it's fairly clear. We would like to do this.

C: Thank you for understanding and cooperation. You just put the bag on the conveyor belt, and your laptop, watch, keys and other metal articles in the tray. Then, you walk through this gate and collect them at the other end of the desk.

P: Cool. Thanks a lot.

C: It's my pleasure.

3.4.2.3   There is also a special passage over there

(C: Clerk   GC: Ground Clerk)

Setting: A ground crew pushes a wheelchair-bound passenger to the check-in counter.

C: Good morning, Sir.

GC: Good morning, Miss. I'm here to assist this Sir in checking in. He is disabled and needs special assistance.

C: No problem. Can you show me his ticket and passport, please?

GC: Here you are.

C: Is there any baggage to be checked in?

GC: No. He just has a hand luggage.

C: Okay. Here is his passport and boarding pass. His seat is on 1st Row 1D, a special seat for disabled passenger.

GC: Thank you.

C: There is also a special passenger with wheelchair over there. A ground staff will bring him down to the gate, and then be lifted onto the plane.

GC: I see. Thank you again.

P: Thank you for your kindness help, Miss. Goodbye.

C: It's my pleasure. Have a nice trip.

3.4.2.4   Please put your luggage on the conveyor belt

(C: Clerk   P: Passenger)

C: Would you please put your carry-on baggage on the belt?

P: Okay. But I have film in my bag.

C: It doesn't matter. The X-ray machine is not harmful for the film.

P: Thank you.

C: Now please put your watch, keys and metal articles in the tray. Then walk through the detector.

P: Sure. Thank you.

C: Have a nice trip.

3.4.3 Cultural Background

Provisions of the Civil Aviation Administration of China

A. Provisions of Items Prohibited in Both Carry-On and Checked Baggage

The items below are prohibited in both carry-on baggage and checked baggage:

(1) Guns, mechanical appliances for military or police use (including main parts and components) and their imitations.

(2) Explosive objects such as ammunition, fireworks, blasting equipment and their imitations.

(3) Controlled knives.

(4) Flammable and explosive items, such as matches, lighters (gas), alcohol, paint, gasoline, kerosene, benzene, rosin oil, tobacco cake, etc.

(5) Corrosive substances, such as hydrochloric acid, sulfuric acid, nitric acid, liquid storage batteries, etc.

(6) Toxic or harmful products, such as cyanide, toxic pesticides, etc.

(7) Radioactive substances, such as radioactive isotopes, etc.

(8) Other objects harmful to aviation safety, such as ferromagnetic objects, which may disturb aircraft instrumentation, and objects with strong pungent odors.

B. Provisions of Items Prohibited in Carry-On Baggage but Permitted in Checked Baggage

The items below are prohibited in carry-on baggage but permitted in checked baggage on domestic flights:

(1) Kitchen knives, clippers, big fruit knives, razors and other knives for daily use.

(2) Professional knives, including surgical knives, sticking knives, gravers, etc.

(3) Knives, spears, swords, and other similar items used for performances.

(4) Sports goods harmful to aviation safety or personal security, such as aggravated canes, canes with sharp nails, alpenstocks, baseball bats, etc.

(5) Axes, chisels, hammers, awls, spanners and other objects harmful to aviation safety or personal security.

(6) Liquid items which exceed type or amount limitations for carry-on baggage.

C. Provisions of Liquid Items

a. International & Regional Flights Provisions of the Civil Aviation Administration of China

(1) The volume of each container of liquid items carried by passengers on international and regional flights departing from domestic airports should not exceed 100 milliliters. If the volume of the container exceeds 100 ml, regardless of whether the container is full or not, it must be checked. Containers of liquid items should be packed in a transparent plastic bag that can be re-sealed. The volume of the bag should be no more than 1 liter. Each passenger can carry only one bag on one flight. Bags that exceed the limitations should be checked. For transparent plastic bags with liquid items, security checks should be done separately.

(2) Goods purchased on the flights or in duty-free shops at the airport should be packed in sealed transparent plastic bags. The bags should not be opened by the passengers. Shopping receipts must be kept for inspection.

(3) A certain amount of liquid dairy products for passengers with babies and essential liquid medicine for diabetic patients or other patients can be carried along with the passengers after security check.

(4) Passengers violating the above provisions are responsible for all consequences.

b. Domestic Flights Provisions of the Civil Aviation Administration of China

(1) Passengers on domestic flights are not allowed to carry on liquids, but liquids may be carried in checked luggage in accordance with relevant packaging provisions.

(2) Passengers may carry a small amount of cosmetics for personal use on the journey. Only one container of each category can be carried with the passengers. The volume should not exceed 100 ml. The containers should be packed separately and go through open-bottle inspections.

(3) Passengers transferring from international flights are allowed to carry duty-free liquid items with receipts that are packed in sealed transparent plastic bags and must go through security checks.

(4) Passengers with babies can apply for free liquid dairy products provided by airline companies when buying tickets. Essential liquid medicines for diabetic patients or other patients can be kept by aircrew after security check.

(5) Passengers violating the above provisions are responsible for all consequences.

D. Relevant regulations on lighters and matches

It is forbidden for passengers (including international flights / regional flights, domestic flights) to carry any lighter or match, either in carry-on or check-in baggage.

E. Regulations on carrying lithium batteries on flights

It is prescribed by the CAAC that:

(1) Lithium batteries can only be taken onto planes as carry-on rather than checked baggage.

(2) Passengers can carry electronic products that incorporate lithium / lithium-ion battery cells or batteries. Such devices must be intended only for private use (such as watches, calculators, mobile phones, laptop computers and portable video cameras).

(3) Lithium batteries must be protected from short circuit and can only be taken as carry-on

baggage. Each passenger can carry two standby batteries at most.

3.5 Accident Solution

3.5.1 Language Points and Useful Sentence Patterns

3.5.1.1 Language Points

1. scissors

A small device for trimming eyebrows.

2. storage period

The service of the airport provides for passengers to store their personal items.

3. limitation

The maximum volume for liquid products.

4. Lighter

A device for lighting, igniting fuel, charges or fires, prohibited to bring on to the aircraft.

3.5.1.2 Useful Sentence Patterns

1. Expressing Prohibited

You are not allowed to...

I won't let you...

You don't have the right to...

You are prohibited to...

2. Expressing Request

May I see...?

Would you mind showing me...?

Would you do me a favor, please?

Could you please show me...?

I was wondering if you could help me.

3. Asking for Permission

Do you mind if I take it away?

May I have permission to...?

Would you allow me...?

You don't mind if I put down the shade, do you?

I was wondering if I could put the bag on the belt.

Could you spare me a few minutes?

Would it be all right if I put my hand baggage here?

3.5.2   Dialogues

3.5.2.1   You need clean up your baggage and redo the security check

(C: Clerk   P: Passenger)

C: Excuse me, Miss. Would you please put your handbag on the belt? And go through the gate.

P: Yes, Sir.

C: Sorry, Miss. There is probably a sharp metal article in your bag. Can you please clean up your baggage and redo the security check.

P: No problem.

Setting: The lady goes back and redoes the security check.

C: Miss, there is a little scissors in your bag. I'm afraid you can't take it on board.

P: Oh, it's one of my beauty accessories. How should I do with it?

C: According to the regulation, you have two options. You can check your luggage out and put it to your checked baggage. Or you have to dispose of it.

P: Okay. Just take it away. I will buy a new one.

C: Thank your for cooperation. You can leave now.

P: Thank you very much.

3.5.2.2   The storage period is only one month

(C: Clerk   P: Passenger)

C: Excuse me, Miss. Could you please come over for a while?

P: What's the matter?

C: There is a liquid article in your bag. Can you take it out for second check, please?

P: Okay, here you are.

C: Sorry, Miss. This container is over the limitation. I'm afraid you can't bring it on board.

P: I don't know this limitation before.

C: The container over 100 mile liters can't be taken on board.

P: Okay, but how should I do with it now?

C: You can store it here.

P: How long will it be stored?

C: The storage period is only one month.

P: I think it would be enough. Thank you for your assistance.

C: It's my pleasure.

3.5.2.3   There is something wrong with your ticket

(C: Clerk   P:Passenger)

P: Good afternoon, Sir.

C: Good afternoon. May I have your ticket and passport, please?

P: Here you are.

C: Sorry, Sir. There is something wrong with your ticket. The information on your ticket doesn't match the one on the passport.

P: What's the wrong with my ticket?

C: The character of your given name is not the same as the one on your passport.

P: Really. Let me have a look at it.

C: Here you are.

P: Thank you. I think it maybe the travel agent made the mistake when they bought the ticket for me. What should I do now?

C: You can call the travel agent to refund the ticket and issue a new one.

P: Thank you very much. I will do it right now.

3.5.2.4　We must open and check your bag

(C: Clerk　P: Passenger)

C: Excuse me, Sir. We must open and check your bag.

P: That's okay. What's the wrong with my bag?

C: There is a lighter in your bag. According to the CAAC's regulation, you can't take it into the passenger cabin.

P: Sorry, Sir. I don't know this before.

C: It doesn't matter. We have to dispose it.

P: Thank you so much.

3.5.3　Cultural Background

Issues concerning bringing liquid articles on domestic flights

(1) Only a small amount of cosmetics (shampoo and body shampoo excluded) intended for personal travel use, one bottle of each variety, can be allowed to be carried onto the plane. The volume of each container must be limited to 100 ml. All should be placed in an independent bag and will be opened / unsealed for inspection. Pay attention to the following items when you prepare for your trip: If the cosmetics are not to be used during the flight, please put them in check-in baggage. If a cosmetic container is larger than 100 ml, please change it into one smaller than 100 ml, or put it in your check-in baggage. In case the cosmetic is intended as a gift and not to be unsealed, please put it in check-in baggage because all carry-on cosmetics must be opened for inspection. Alcoholic drinks are prohibited to be taken as carry-on and must be put in check-in baggage.

(2) If you have a baby, please report it to the airline company when you are buying tickets. The company will offer liquid dairy products for free. As liquid dairy products are prohibited for carry-on, please put them in check-in baggage, or dispose of them yourself before entering

security inspection.

(3) Diabetes sufferers or other patients may carry necessary liquid products with them, such as liquid medicine and liquid sugar-free food, but only in dosages sufficient for use during the flight. A certificate provided by either a hospital or a doctor is required in such a case.

(4) Passengers who are transferring from international to domestic flights, and are carrying duty-free liquid articles bought abroad, should put the liquid within a sealed, unimpaired, transparent bag, and be prepared to show the shopping voucher. If the bag holding the sealed liquid article is impaired, or no shopping voucher is available, you will not be allowed to board domestic flights unless the volume and category of your liquid article complies with relevant regulations for domestic flights.

(5) Passengers with any liquid articles outside the above cases that are indefinable should put them in check-in baggage.

Unit 4
Welcome Aboard

4.1　Seat Arrangement

4.1.1　Language Points and Useful Sentence Patterns

4.1.1.1　Language Points

1. aisle

A way between lines of seats in the cabin of aircraft.

2. overhead compartment

Other names for it are "overhead bin" or "overhead locker". It refers to the place where passengers hand baggage is stowed on an airplane.

3. call button

It is a button located on a panel on the inside armrest of passengers' seats or beneath the overhead bin. A passenger presses it to get the button of the CAs.

4. window seat

Window seat is a bench or similar seat built into a window recess.

5. seat belt

A safety belt used in a plane to hold you in your seat during taking-off and landing in case of an accident.

4.1.1.2　Useful Sentence Patterns

1. Offering / Asking for Help

Do you need any help?

Is there anything I can do for you?

Could you do me a favor?

Could you come over and help me out?

2. Expressing Likes and Dislikes

I don't like it.

I feel like a glass of spring water now.

I'm crazy about jazz music.

It would be nice to have some.

I can't find words to express how much I like it.

3. Expressing Instructions

First of all you should remember to do that.

Let me show you, first... then... after that... And finally…

The following procedures should be adopted.

Look, you have to do this.

You should do it like this: press the button and lean back at the same time.

4.1.2　Dialogues

4.1.2.1　Could you direct me to my seat?

(A: Attendant　P: Passenger)

A: Good morning, Sir. Welcome aboard.

P: Good morning. Where is my seat?

A: Could you show me your boarding pass, please?

P: Here you are.

A: Your seat number is 25C. It's in the middle of the cabin, the one by the aisle.

P: It's my first time to travel by plane. I don't know where I can find the seat number. Could you direct me to my seat, please?

A: Sure. Please go along the aisle. The seat number is on the edge of the overhead compartment. Here is your seat.

P: Thank you very much.

A: It's my pleasure.

P: If you need any help, please press the call button.

A: Okay, thanks a lot.

4.1.2.2　Would you please go back to your assigned seat for the time being?

(A: Attendant　P: Passenger)

P1: Excuse me, where is my seat?

A: May I see your boarding pass, please? I will show you where your seat is.

P1: Here it is.

A: Your seat is 30A, the window seat.

Setting: Passenger is going to his seat, but he found that his seat was occupied by a man.

P1: Excuse me, Miss, my seat has been taken by someone. Could you come and help, please?

A: Excuse me, Sir. Can you show me your boarding pass, please?

P2: Of course. My seat number is 30C.

A: I am sorry. You may take a wrong seat. 30C is the aisle seat. Would you please go back to your assigned seat for the time being?

P2: Sure. Sorry about that.

A: Thank you for your cooperation. Have a good trip.

4.1.2.3　Could you help me with the seat?

(A: Attendant　P: Passenger)

Setting: A cabin attendant is looking over in the cabin.

A: Excuse me, Sir. Could you please return your seat back to the upright position?

P1: Yes, but how can I return it back?

A: Let me show you. You can adjust your seat back by pulling this release button on the side of the arm rest. Once you pull it, you'll be able to return your seat back to the upright position.

P1: Okay, let me try. Cool, it is working well. Thank you very much.

A: Well done. If you need any help, please press the call button.

P1: Certainly.

Setting: Then there is another passenger having trouble with the seat belt.

C: Morning, Madam. How can I help you?

P2: Hi, Miss. I don't know how to fasten my seat belt. Could you give me a hand?

A: Sure. Firstly, you can put this metal insert into the buckle, and then pull on the loose end to tighten the belt around your waist.

P2: Okay, I got it. Thanks a lot.

4.1.3   Cultural Background

Pre-flight Safety Demonstration

The pre-flight safety briefing (also known as a pre-flight demonstration, in-flight safety briefing, in-flight safety demonstration, safety instructions, or simply the safety video) is a detailed explanation given before take-off to airline passengers about the safety features of the aircraft they are aboard.

Aviation regulations do not state how an airline should deliver the briefing, only that "The operator of an aircraft shall ensure that all passengers are orally briefed before each take-off". As a result, and depending on the in-flight entertainment system in the aircraft, as well as the airline's policy, airlines may deliver a pre-recorded briefing or provide a live demonstration. A live demonstration is performed by a flight attendant standing up in the aisle, while another flight attendant narrates over the public address system. A pre-recorded briefing may feature audio only, or may take the form of a video (audio plus visual). Pre-flight safety briefings will typically last two to six minutes. In consideration for travelers not speaking the airline's official language and for the passengers with hearing problems, the video may feature subtitles, an on-screen signer, or may be repeated in another language.

Some safety videos are made using three-dimensional graphics. Other videos were made to be humorous, or feature celebrities, or were based on popular movies. Many safety videos were uploaded to YouTube. Cebu Pacific choreographed the entire demonstration to Lady Gaga's "Just Dance" and Katy Perry's "California Gurls" as an experiment during one of their flights. The flight attendant featured in the most recent Delta Air Lines video has become an internet celebrity known as Deltalina.

In an emergency, flight attendants are trained to calmly instruct passengers how to respond, given the type of emergency. Research conducted at the University of New South Wales Australia questions the effectiveness of these briefings in conveying key safety messages for passengers to recall and act upon in an emergency. In one study, a range of pre-recorded safety briefings were tested. One safety briefing contained humor, another was void of humor (said to reflect a standard style briefing), and another used a celebrity to sell the importance of the safety briefing and the messages contained within. Not long after being exposed to the briefing, individuals recalled approximately 50% of the key safety messages from the briefing featuring the celebrity, 45% from the briefing containing humor, and 32% from the briefing void of both a celebrity and humor. Two hours post exposure to the pre-flight safety briefings, recall decreased on average by 4% from the original levels across all conditions.

4.2　Baggage Arrangement

4.2.1　Language Points and Useful Sentence Patterns

4.2.1.1　Language Points

1. fragile items

Items are easily broken or damaged or destroyed.

2. emergency exit

A permits exit in the case of fire or other emergency.

4.2.1.2　Useful Sentence Patterns

1. Expressing Uncertainty

I don't know where I should put my baggage.

I am not sure...

It is hard to say...

It is difficult to say...

2. Reply appreciation

You're welcome.

It's my pleasure.

That's all right.

No worries.

Don't mention is too much.

Not at all.

3. Expressing Interrupting

Excuse me.

I'm sorry to interrupt you.

Could you please come for a while?

Could you spare me a few minutes?

4.2.2　Dialogues

4.2.2.1　Where should I put my baggage?

(A: Attendant　P: Passenger)

A: Excuse me, Miss. I don't know where I should put my baggage. The overhead compartment is full.

P: There is more room in the front cabin. If you don't mind, I can put your baggage there.

A: No problem. There are some fragile items in my bag. Please take extra care about it.

P: Okay, I will. I will bring it back to you when disembark.

A: Thank you very much.

P: You are welcome.

4.2.2.2　The overhead compartment couldn't be closed.

(A: Attendant　P: Passenger)

Setting: There is a passenger pressing the call button.

A: Excuse me, Miss. Did you press the call button?

P: Yes. I stowed my baggage in the overhead compartment. But it couldn't be closed.

A: Let me have a look. Ah, your bag is too big to fit the overhead bin. Why don't you place it under your seat?

P: Yes, I tried. But it doesn't fit as well.

A: Well...er... let me see. Can you try to put it under the seat in front of you.

P: Okay, let me try again. Yeah, it does fit eventually.

A: That's great. Hope you enjoy your trip.

P: Thanks a lot. That's very kind of you.

A: Don't mention it too much.

4.2.2.3　The emergency exit must not be blocked during the flight

(A: Attendant　P: Passenger)

Setting: The cabin attendant is doing inspection in the cabin. Then she found that there is a baggage blocking the emergency exit.

A: Excuse me, whose baggage is it?

P: It's mine. What's the problem?

A: I'm afraid you can't leave your bag on the aisle. According the CAAC's regulation, the emergency exit must not be blocked during the flight.

P: I'm sorry. But I don't know where to put it.

C: Could you please put it in the overhead compartment?

P: Well, I have tried. But the overhead compartment is over full.

C: Don't you mind me taking it to the front cabin and look after it for you?

P: It seems there is no better choice than this. Thank you very much.

C: You are welcome.

4.2.3   Cultural Background

System Safety and Regulation

One major obstacle in creating an in-flight entertainment system is system safety. With the sometimes miles of wiring involved, voltage leaks and arcing become a problem. This is of more than theoretical concern. The IFE system was implicated in the crash of Swissair Flight 111 in 1998. To contain any possible issues, the in-flight entertainment system is typically isolated from the main systems of the aircraft. In the United States, for a product to be considered safe and reliable, it must be certified by the FAA and pass all of the applicable requirements found in the Federal Aviation Regulations. The concerning section, or title, dealing with the aviation industry and the electronic systems embedded in the aircraft, is CFR title 14 parts 25. Contained inside Part 25 are rules relating to the aircraft's electronic system.

There are two major sections of the FAA's airworthiness regulations that regulate flight entertainment systems and their safety in transport category aircraft: 14 CFR 25.1301 which approves the electronic equipment for installation and use, by assuring that the system in question is properly labeled, and that its design is appropriate to its intended function.14 CFR 25.1309 states that the electrical equipment must not alter the safety or functionality of the aircraft upon the result of a failure. One way for the intended IFE system to meet this regulatory requirement is for it to be independent from the aircraft's main power source and processor. By separating the power supplies and data links from that of the aircraft's performance processor, in the event of a failure the system is self-sustained, and can not alter the functionality of the aircraft. Upon a showing of compliance to all of the applicable U.S. regulations the in-flight entertainment system is capable of being approved in the United States. Certain U.S. design approvals for IFE may be directly accepted in other countries, or may be capable of being validated, under existing bilateral airworthiness safety agreements.

4.3   Food Service

4.3.1   Language Points and Useful Sentence Patterns

4.3.1.1   Language Points

1. tray table

A small table fixed on the front seat or stowed inside the armrest.

2. main course

The main course is the main dish of a multi-dish meal. The main course can also be called the entree.

3. hors d'oeuvre

Small appetizers served before the meal. It can be cold or hot. They are usually one-or two-bite-size pieces of food. "hors d'oeuvre" is properly used for both the singular and plural forms.

4. Halva

Halva is made of powder, sesame seeds, peanuts, and raisin. It is a typical Indian food.

4.3.1.2 Useful Sentence Patterns

1. Providing Suggestion

Would you like to have...?

Do you mind to try...?

Do you think...?

2. Expressing Waiting

Please wait for a while.

Please wait a moment.

Please give me few minutes.

I will be back in a minute.

I will be back very soon.

3. Expressing "We have"

We prepare...

We can offer you...

We can provide you...

...are available.

4.3.2 Dialogues

4.3.2.1 Could you get me something to drink?

(A: Attendant   P: Passenger)

P: Excuse me, Miss. May I have something to drink?

A: Of course.

P: What kind of drinks do you have?

A: We have tea, coffee, beer, Sprite, Seven Up, Coco Cola, fruit juice and mineral water. What would you like?

P: I'd like fruit juice. What kind of fruit juice do you have?

A: We offer apple juice, orange juice and grape juice.

P: I prefer a cup of orange juice, please?

A: Okay, here is your orange juice.

P: Thank you very much.

A: You are welcome.

4.3.2.2   What would you like for dinner?

(A: Attendant   P: Passenger)

A: We are going to serve dinner now. Would you please pull down the tray table?

P: Okay. What is the main course?

A: We prepare chicken with rice and beef steak.

P: I'd like beef steak with medium rare, please.

A: All right. One minute, please. Would you like to have red wine to go with the steak?

P: Great. It will be perfect. Thank you very much.

A: Enjoy your dinner.

4.3.2.3   Have you mentioned your specific diets when you booked the ticket?

(A: Attendant   P: Passenger)

P: Miss, I can not eat all the food on this menu. I'm a vegetarian. Do you have a special meal for me?

A: Have you mentioned your specific diets when you booked the ticket?

P: Yes, I have. I ordered a vegetarian meal when I booked the ticket.

A: Okay, can I have your name please? I will check in the galley.

P: My name is Adam Black.

A: Okay, wait for a minute.

P: Thanks a lot.

Setting: Few minutes later.

A: Excuse me, Sir. Here is the vegetarian meal you ordered. That's vegetable hors d'oeuvre and vegetable soup.

P: Great. Would you mind giving me some Halva, and a cup of water?

A: Please wait a moment.

4.3.2.4   May I clear up your table now?

(A: Attendant   P: Passenger)

A: Excuse me, Madam. May I clear up your table now?

P: Yes, please. By the way, can I have a cup of tea?

A: What kind of tea would like?

P: What do you have?

A: We prepare green tea, black tea, jasmine tea and rose tea. What would you like?

P: I like a cup of rose tea, please.

A: Sure. Please wait for a moment.

P: No problem.

4.3.3　Cultural Background

Airline Meal

The type of food varies depending upon the Airline Company and class of travel. Meals may be served on one tray or in multiple courses with no tray and with a tablecloth, metal cutlery, and glassware (generally in first and business classes). Often the food is reflective of the culture of the country the airline is based in.

The airline dinner typically includes meat (most commonly chicken or beef), fish, or pasta; a salad or vegetable; a small bread roll; and a dessert. Condiments (typically salt pepper and sugar) are supplied in small sachets or shakers.

Caterers usually produce alternative meals for passengers with restrictive diets. These must usually be ordered in advance, sometimes when buying the ticket. Some of the more common examples include: cultural diets, such as Turkish, French, Italian, Chinese, Korean, Japanese or Indian style.

Infant and baby meals: Some airlines also offer children's meals, containing foods that children will enjoy such as baked beans, mini-hamburgers and hot dogs. Medical diets, including low / high fiber, low fat / cholesterol, diabetic, peanut free, non-lactose, low salt / sodium, low-calorie, low-protein, bland (non-spicy) and gluten-free meals.

Religious diets include kosher, halal, and Hindu, Buddhist and Jain vegetarian (sometimes termed Asian vegetarian) meals.

Vegetarian and vegan meals. Some airlines do not offer a specific meal for non-vegan vegetarians; instead, they are given a vegan meal.

4.4　In-flight Service

4.4.1　Language Points and Useful Sentence Patterns

4.4.1.1　Language Points

1. release button

The button can be used to adjust the seat back.

2. reading light

Reading light is located on the bottom of the overhead compartment.

3. headset

A receiver consisting of a pair of headphones.

4. first-aid kit

A kit consists of a set of bandages and medicines for giving first aid.

5. alternative landing

Aircraft cannot or should not be landing at the airport of destination or destination are not suitable for landing, and landed at another airport is known as an alternative landing.

6. nitroglycerin

A heavy yellow poisonous oily explosive liquid obtains nitrating glycerol; used in making explosives and medically as a vasodilator.

4.4.1.2   Useful Sentence Patterns

1. Asking for Agreement or Approval

Do you agree with me on this point?

Is it OK now?

Don't you feel it will work?

Would you concur with such a proposal?

Have I got it right?

Would you agree with what I said just now?

2. Expressing Agreement

I quite agree with you.

I'm very pleased about you arrangement.

That's a good idea.

I suppose so.

That's an excellent idea.

3. Making Suggestions

Would you like a cup of coffee?

Shall we go there and look for a vacant seat?

Would you care for another cup of coffee?

How about having rice with beef?

Why don't you try this new red wine?

4.4.2   Dialogues

4.4.2.1   Would you please return your seat back to the upright position?

Setting: A flight attendant comes around to do the normal pre-flight safety check.

A: Excuse me, Sir. Would you please return your seat back to the upright position? For your safety, the seat back should be kept in the upright position during taking-off and landing.

P: I'm sorry, but I don't know how to do it.

A: There is a release button on the side of the arm rest. You can use it to adjust your seat. If you push it, the seat back slides backward and reclines, so you can relax and be comfortable.

P: That's very kind of you.

A: It's my pleasure.

4.4.2.2 Offering newspapers and magazines

P: Excuse me, Miss. I feel bit boring. Can I have something to read?

A: That's okay. We have China Daily, People's Daily, Financial Report and Discovery. What would you like?

P: I'd like China Daily, please.

A: Okay, here you are.

P: Thank you very much.

A: By the way, you'd better to turn on the reading light which is over your head on the bottom of the overhead compartment.

P: I really appreciated your help.

4.4.2.3 Can I have a headset?

Setting: In the cabin, there is a passenger pressed the call button.

A: Morning, Sir. Can I help you?

P: Excuse me, Miss. I'd like to listen to the music. Can I have a headset, please?

A: Sure. Here you are.

P: I'd like to listen to music. I don't know how to use it. Can you help me to adjust it?

A: No problem. We provide several kinds of music, pop music, classical music and jazz. Which would you prefer?

P: I like pop music.

C: Okay, please choose the first channel. And you can adjust the volume by pressing the volume button up or down.

P: Thank you very much for your help.

C: No worries.

4.4.2.4 Do you have any medicine with you?

Setting: A passenger presses the call button and a cabin crew comes over.

P: Sorry, Miss. I'm feeling dismayed and dizzy. Could you please give me a cup of water?

C: No problem. One moment, please.

Setting: When the stewardess comes back, the passenger is losing consciousness.

C: Hello, Sir. Are you okay? Can you hear me? Do you have any medicine with you?

Setting: The passenger is in a coma. Other cabin crew and the purser come over to help.

Purser: I'll check his pocket to see if there's any medicine. Marry, bring the first-aid kit please. Lucy, you make an announcement to see if there is a doctor or a nurse on board and report to the captain that we may have to make an alternative landing.

Setting: Meanwhile, the purser finds a little bottle of nitroglycerin. A doctor joins the purser and cabin crew.

D: He seems to be having a heart attack. Put a pill of nitroglycerin under his tongue. Loosen his tied and coat right now, and keep his airway clean.

Setting: Three minutes later, the passenger comes to himself.

P: It's very glad to see you people again.

C: I hope you are feeling better, Sir. We'll divert to a nearby airport. The ambulance is waiting on the apron and the doctors will examine you when you disembark. I believe you will be recovered in no time.

P: Thank you all. You've just saved my life.

4.4.2.5   Serving a passenger with a baby

Setting: Setting: After dinner, captain turn down the light and passengers are going to sleep. Then there is a baby keeping crying in the middle of the cabin.

A: Excuse me, Miss. What's wrong with your little baby?

P: Oh, I think she is hungry. I need some hot water to prepare some milk for her.

A: Okay, I will get some for you now. Please wait a moment.

P: Thank you very much. I also need some tissues.

A: No problem at all. I will be back soon. If you need any other help, please press the call button.

4.4.3   Cultural Background

History of In-flight Entertainment

The first in-flight movie was in 1921 on Aeromarine Airways showing a film called Howdy Chicago to its passengers as the amphibious airplane flew around Chicago. The film The Lost World was shown to passengers of an Imperial Airways flight in April 1925 between London (Croydon Airport) and Paris.

Eleven years later in 1932, the first in-flight television called "media event" was shown on a Western Air Express Fokker F.10 aircraft. The post-WWII British Bristol Brabazon airliner was initially specified with a 37-seat cinema within its huge fuselage; this was later reduced to a 23-seat cinema sharing the rear of the aircraft with a lounge and cocktail bar. The aircraft never entered service.

However, it was not until the 1960s that in-flight entertainment (other than reading, sitting in a lounge and talking, or looking out the window) was becoming mainstream and popular. In 1961, David Flexor of In-flight Motion Pictures developed the 16mm film system using a 25-inch reel for a wide variety of commercial aircraft. Capable of holding the entire film, and mounted horizontally to maximize space, this replaced the previous 30-inch-diameter film reels. In 1961, TWA committed to Flexor's technology and was first to debut a feature film in flight. Interviewed by the New Yorker in 1962, Mr. Flexner said, "an awful lot of ingenuity has gone into this thing, which started from my simply thinking one day, in flight, that air travel is both the most advanced form of transportation and the most boring." Amerlon Productions, a subsidiary of In-flight, produced at least one film, Deadlier Than the Male, specifically for use on airplanes.

In 1963, AVID Airline Products developed and manufactured the first pneumatic headset used on board the airlines and provided these early headsets to TWA. These early systems consisted of in-seat audio that could be heard with hollow tube headphones. In 1979 pneumatic headsets were replaced by electronic headsets. The electronic headsets were initially available only on selected flights and premium cabins whereas economy class still had to make do with the old pneumatic headsets.[citation needed] In the United States, the last airline to offer pneumatic headphones was Delta Air Lines, which switched to electronic headphones in 2003, despite the fact that all Delta aircraft equipped with in-flight entertainment since the Boeing 767-200 have included jacks for electronic headphones.

Throughout the early to mid-1960s, some in-flight movies were played back from videotape, using early compact transistorized videotape recorders made by Sony (such as the SV-201 and PV-201) and Ampex (such as the VR-660 and VR-1500), and played back on CRT monitors mounted on the upper sides in the cabin above the passenger seats with several monitors placed a few seats apart from each other. The audio was played back through the headsets.

In 1971, TRANSCOM developed the 8mm film cassette. Flight attendants could now change movies in-flight and add short subject programming.

In the late 1970s and early 1980s, CRT-based projectors began to appear on newer wide body aircraft, such as the Boeing 767. These used LaserDiscs or video cassettes for playback. Some airlines upgraded the old film IFE systems to the CRT-based systems in the late 1980s and early 1990s on some of their older wide bodies. In 1985, Avicom introduced the first audio player system, based on the Philips Tape Cassette technology. In 1988, the Air vision company introduced the first in-seat audio / video on-demand systems using 2.7 inches (69 mm) LCD technology for Northwest Airlines. The trials, which were run by Northwest Airlines on its Boeing 747 fleet, received overwhelmingly positive passenger reaction. As a result, this completely replaced the CRT technology.

Today, in-flight entertainment is offered as an option on almost all wide body aircraft, while some narrow body aircraft are not equipped with any form of In-flight entertainment at all. This is mainly due to the aircraft storage and weight limits. The Boeing 757 was the first narrow body aircraft to widely feature both audio and video In-flight entertainment and today it is rare to find a Boeing 757 without an In-flight entertainment system. Most Boeing 757s feature ceiling-mounted CRT screens, although some newer 757s may feature drop-down LCDs or audio-video on demand systems in the back of each seat. Many Airbus A320series and Boeing 737 Next Generation aircraft are also equipped with drop-down LCD screens. Some airlines, such as WestJet, United Airlines, and Delta Air Lines, have equipped some narrow body aircraft with personal video screens at every seat. Others, such as Air Canada and JetBlue, have even equipped some regional with AVOD.

For the introduction of personal TVs onboard jetBlue, company management tracked that lavatory queuing went far down. They originally had two planes; one with functioning IFE and one with none, the functioning one later was called "the happy plane".

4.5　Special Service in Flight

4.5.1　Language Points and Useful Sentence Patterns

4.5.1.1　Language Points

1. airsick

Airsick is experiencing motion sickness.

2. unruly passenger

Passenger is noisy and lacking in restraint or discipline.

3. local time

The official time in a local region (adjusted for location around the Earth); established by law or custom.

4.5.1.2　Useful Sentence Patterns

1. Expressing Refusal

I'm sorry I can't.

I can't do it right now, but maybe later.

I'm sorry, but I have an emergency to attend to.

I'm trying to focus on finishing off some other things.

2. Expressing Apology

I can't tell you how sorry I am.

Words cannot describe how sorry I am.

You cannot believe how sorry I am.

I just don't know what to say.

3. Expressing Concern

I'm deeply sorry to hear that.

What's the matter with you, Miss?

Let me help you lie down.

Are you all right now?

Would you like me to do anything for you?

4.5.2　Dialogues

4.5.2.1　Helping a sick passenger on board

(A: Attendant　P: Passenger)

A: I'm feeling dizzy and nausea.

P: Did you press the call button, Miss? What's the matter?

A: Yes. I also feel like throwing up.

P: You look pale. Is this your first time to travel by plane?

A: Oh, my God. I have no idea about it. So what can I do?

P: From my experience you are probably airsick.

A: Your hot water and tablet, please. You'd better take a nap after take the medicine.

P: Don't worry. We have airsick tablets on board. I'll bring some for you.

A: It's my pleasure.

P: Thank you very much. It's very kind of you.

4.5.2.2   Serving for an unruly passenger

(A: Attendant   P: Passenger)

Setting: A man and a lady with her little girl have asked for a blanket, but there is only one available. The cabin attendant gives the last one to the little girl.

P: Excuse me, Miss. I asked you for a blanket. But now it was over twenty minutes past. I still have not gotten it. What's the problem with you?

A: Oh, I am sorry, Sir. There is also another lady with a little girl asking for the blanket. I just gave it to that lady because there is only one left. I am awfully sorry about ignoring you.

P: That's too bad. I have be waiting here for nearly half an hour. Even there is no one of your cabin attendants come to serve me during that time. How were you guys doing your job properly?

A: Please accept my sincere apology for my careless. The little children need more attention, while there is actually no more blankets. I hope you could understand. If you feel cold, I can tell the captain to turn down the air conditioner to increase the temperature in the cabin.

P: Okay, forget it. But I'm not happy. I'll write a letter to complain to your company.

4.5.2.3   Taking care of a passenger's pet

(C: Clerk   P: Passenger)

C: Excuse me. Whose baggage is this?

P: It's mine. What's the matter with it?

C: Madam, would you please put your baggage into the overhead compartment? It blocks the aisle.

P: Sorry about that. But it's not my luggage. It's my service dog.

C: I see. So can I help you put it under your seat, please?

P: I just tried to put it under there. But the cage is too big to fit into the space down there.

C: Then do you mind me taking it to the front cabin?

P: No, I don't if it is the only choice. But please take care of it. And please bring it back to me before landing. I need his help.

C: No problem, Madam.

4.5.2.4　Providing information about hotels

(C: Clerk　P: Passenger)

P: Excuse me, Miss. Can you come over for a while?

C: Sure. What can I help you, Sir?

P: Do you know what the local time is?

C: Yes, Sir. It's half past 5 in the afternoon now. What else can I do for you?

P: I will be staying in Beijing for 3 days on a business trip. Can you recommend some good hotels in the downtown?

C: I'm glad to help you. Where are you planning to stay?

P: I travel here for an International Telecommunication Equipment Expo. Is there any good hotel near it?

C: Certainly yes. There are some international brand hotels near the China International Exhibition Center. You can just directly go there after landing.

P: That's really helpful. Thank you very much.

C: No worries.

4.5.2.5　Helping passengers losing property on board

(A: Attendant　P: Passenger)

P: Hello, Miss.

A: Yes, how can I help you?

P: I can't find my wallet; I had it when I was walking to the toilet, but it's gone when I was back.

A: I'm sorry to hear that. Could you please think about where you saw it before you left you seat?

P: I had kept it in my pocket before I went to the toilet.

A: Have you walked back to you seat and see if you have dropped it?

P: Yes, but there is nothing on my seat.

A: Okay, please go together with me to your seat to have a careful check.

P: That's great. Thank you very much.

Setting: Few minutes later, the attendant found the wallet under the seat.

A: Good luck, Sir. Here is your wallet. It's under the seat.

P: Fortunately you found it. There are all of my identification card and bank cards in it. Thank you so much.

A: You're welcome.

4.5.3　Cultural Background

First Aid Kits on Airline Flights

First aid kits on airline flights are adequate to respond to most in-flight emergencies. However, if you want to take a travel first aid kit with you to your destination, you may want to keep it in checked baggage or you must remove banned first aid items from your kit. Here is a list of approved first aid items that travelers can carry on airline flights.

(1) Allowed on Domestic Airline Flights

Most first aid items are relatively soft and not very dangerous to the average flight crew.

Those items are still welcome in carry-on baggage for domestic airline flights in the United States. Flights overseas have, in most cases, banned all except essential items from carry-on bags. The approved first aid items for domestic airline flights include:

gauze pads,

bandage scissors (blades less than four inches),

roller gauze,

tape,

gloves,

triangular bandages,

elastic bandages,

adhesive bandages,

pain relievers,

moleskin,

lip balms,

barrier devices for CPR.

(2) Allowed in Limited Quantities on Airline Flights

Heightened security on airline flights has led to restrictions on all liquids and gels. Solid items are still available, such as stick antiperspirants or lip balms. Here are restricted items commonly found in a first aid kit:

hand cleaner,

hydrogen peroxide,

antibiotic ointment,

insect bite swabs.

None of these liquids or gels can be in a container larger than 3 fl. oz. (100 ml) and all liquids and gels must fit into a single quart-sized resalable baggie.

4.6　Pre-Landing

4.6.1　Language Points and Useful Sentence Patterns

4.6.1.1　Language Points

1. turbulence

Turbulence is instability in the atmosphere.

2. disembarkation card

It is immigration application forms that people must fill in when they enter a foreign country.

3. Window shades

The white boards on the window of the aircraft are used to shade light.

4.6.1.2 Useful Sentence Patterns

1. Expressing "I don't know"

What are you talking about?

My brain doesn't work.

I have no ides what that is.

What's the point?

This is over my head.

2. Expressing Possibility

It may be that ...

It's likely that ...

It's possible that ...

It's probable that ...

The probability is that ...

3. Expressing Doubt

Are you sure?

Are you serious?

Are you joking?

Do you really mean that?

Are you kidding?

4.6.2 Dialogues

4.6.2.1 Reassuring passengers who feel unsafe

(A: Attendant   P: Passenger)

P: Excuse me, Miss. I was wondering why our flight is keeping bump for quite a few minutes. Is there something wrong with our plane?

A: I don't think so, Madam. Now our flight is landing shortly. Our plane is experiencing turbulence when it is going through the clouds. There is nothing wrong with our plane. Besides, our captain has nearly 30 years flying experience. So there is nothing to be worried about. Trust me. We will be landing safely.

P: Oh, if it is normal, I'm sorry for the fuss.

A: No problem, Madam. I hope you will be all right.

P: Thank you for your patience. You are the most kindly lady I have seen.

4.6.2.2 Completing a disembarkation card

(A: Attendant   P: Passenger)

P: Excuse me, Miss. Here is the disembarkation card. But I am not able to understand what it asks me to do. To be frank, this is my first flight.

A: I'm very glad to help you.

P: For the main reason for my travel, what should I have to say? I am going to visit my daughter.

A: For personal travel, you should tick the "other" box.

P: It also asks me to provide my "Address in Australia"? Should I give my daughter's address here? I will be staying with her.

A: Yes, I think that's what it needs to you to do. According to the Immigration Law, they need to contact you in an emergency.

P: Thank you very much.

A: Please don't forget to write down our flight number in this box. Our flight number is CZ3071.

P: Thanks. You are very helpful.

A: I hope you enjoy your time with your daughter in Australia.

P: Thanks again. I'm sure I will. It would be fantastic if I can take your flight when I return to China.

A: I hope so.

4.6.2.3 Reminding fastening seat belts

Announcement: Ladies and gentleman, our flight will be landing at Guangzhou Bai Yun International Airport in about 30 minutes. Please be seated and fasten your seat belt. Tray tables and seat backs should be returned to the upright position. Window shades must be open. Toilet is going to be closed in 10 minutes, and cabin service will be stopped soon.

Setting: Cabin attendants start to have safety inspection in the cabin. Then there is a passenger sleeping with the seat belt unfastened.

A: Excuse me, Sir. Sorry to interrupt you. Our flight is going to land now. Please fasten you seat belt and return the seat back to the upright position.

P: I'm sorry. I was sleeping just now. I didn't hear the announcement.

A: That's okay. For your safety, please fasten your seat belt and keep the seat back in the upright position. You are able to have a rest later. I will not interrupt you again.

P: Thank you for reminding me.

A: It's my pleasure.

4.6.3 Cultural Background

How to Reduce Jet Lag When Crossing Time Zones

Many experienced travelers are familiar with the feeling of tiredness that accompanies air travel to a foreign location, such as Costa Rica for a surf trip. The body is used to being on a set schedule, and this regulates the person's biological clock. Jet lag is a temporary sleep disorder that impacts an individual's sleep patterns.

There are ways to combat this problem so that more time is spent enjoying your surf trip with us!

You need to drink plenty of water to keep your body properly dehydrated. Traveling to Costa Rica means that you'll be crossing one or more time zones depending on your origin. An airplane will have a highly pressurized environment that will decrease the oxygen available in each traveler blood stream. The lack of oxygen will add to the development of jet lag or tiredness. Water will help to counteract this effect. Prior to leaving, you'll want to drink several glasses of water daily. Water should be also consumed during the flight to prevent dehydration.

It's also recommended that you start to adjust your sleep pattern to more closely match the location that they are visiting. This may require going to bed earlier or staying up later so that the body adjusts to a different sleep rhythm. During the flight, if it's a red eye, you'll want to sleep when it is nighttime. You should also try to remain awake when daylight is streaming into the airplane.

Exercise will also help to reduce the feeling of fatigue when traveling. You'll want to get up whenever possible and walk around the plane, or stretch near your seat.

Eating nutritious meals prior to leaving your destination and when flying on the airplane is also important in fighting off jet lag. Proper planning will help you enjoy your Costa Rica surf trip that much more and help you avoid jet lag so you can get on the waves as soon as you arrive!

Unit 5
Arrival

5.1　Before and After Landing

5.1.1　Language Points and Useful Sentence Patterns

5.1.1.1　Language Points

1. knob

A circular rounded projection or protuberance.

2. tightly

Securely fixed or fastened .

3. stow

Fill by packing tightly.

4. slippery

Causing or tending to cause things to slip or slide.

5. disembark

When passengers disembark from a ship, airplane, or bus, they leave it at the end of their journey.

6. claim

An assertion of a right.

7. reservation

If you have reservations about something, you are not sure that it is entirely good or right.

8. limousine

Any large and luxurious car, esp. one that has a glass division between the driver and passengers.

9. approximately

Close to.

5.1.1.2　Useful Sentence Patterns

Safety Check Jargon

Please bring the seatback to the upright position.

Please open the window shade.

Please fasten your seat belt.

Please retune tray table to the upright position.

5.1.2　Dialogues

5.1.2.1　Make a return flight

(P: Passenger　S: Stewardess)

P: Excuse me, Miss. What is the weather in New York?

S: According to the present weather report, it is snowing heavily. The runway has been covered with two inches snow, and it is impossible for the plane to land. So we are going to fly to Washington.

P: Really, but I have a very import meeting in the afternoon in New York.

S: Don't worry, what time will the meeting begin?

P: Let me check, the meeting will begin at 3 in the afternoon.

S: Our plane will be landing at Washington at 11 in the morning, then you can take High-speed Rail from Washington to New York, you can catch the meeting.

P: OK, thank you very much.

5.1.2.2   Security Check

(P: Passenger   S: Stewardess)

S: Excuse me, Miss. Please bring the seatback to the upright position.

P: Why should I bring the seatback to the upright position? The space is too narrow, I don't feel Comfortable.

S: Because the plane is descending now, if an emergency occurs, it will prevent us from evacuating.

P: OK, I get it, but I do not know how to stow my seatback.

S: Let me help you. Just press this knob and put it upright. Now it is properly. By the way, please open the window shade.

P: OK, I will open it now, oh my God, the scenery is so marvelous. What a beautiful fire cloud!

S: Thank you for your cooperation.

5.1.2.3   Arrival Time

(P: Passenger   S: Stewardess)

P: Miss, could you tell me when we will be landing at Beijing International Airport?

S: We will arrive at Beijing International Airport in 30 minutes. The arrival time is 10:50 a.m.

P: What's the weather like in Beijing?

S: Oh, the weather in Beijing is total different from Sanya, you'd better take more clothes due to the cold weather.

P: OK, thank you very much. Can I use the toilet now?

S: The toilet is still available in 5 minutes due to the plane is descending, please be hurry!

P: OK, thank you very much.

5.1.2.4   Goodbye

(P: Passenger   S: Stewardess)

S: Goodbye, Mr. Black. I hope you enjoy your stay in China, we hope to see you again soon.

P: Thank you for your excellent service. Goodbye for now.

S: Thank you, ma' am. Please watch your steps. It is rather slippery outside.

P: Thank you. Goodbye.

S: Hi, young girl, may I help you down the stairs?

P: Thank you, sister! This is my first flight, and I am very satisfied with your company, next time I will choose your company again.

S: You are welcome. We hope to see you on board again soon.

5.1.2.5　Comprehensive Dialogue

(P: Passenger　S: Stewardess)

S: Excuse me, Madam, please remain in your seat and fasten your seat belt.

P: I know. But I want to gather my bags together and prepare to disembark.

S: Don't worry about it. You will have enough time to collect your belongings. After the plane has come to a complete stop, I will help you with your bags.

P: And could you tell me where the Baggage Claim Area is?

S: The Baggage Claim Area is in the arrival hall. When you arrive, you will see signs to the Baggage Claim Area and Exit. If you follow them you will find your bags.

P: Thank you.

S: Thank you for flying with us and hope to have the pleasure of being with you again.

P: Miss, could you tell me when we will be landing at Beijing Capital International Airport?

S: We will arrive at Beijing Capital International Airport in ten minutes. The arrival time is 6:50 p.m.

P: Thank you. What's the weather like there?

S: According to the latest weather report, it's sunny and the temperature is 20 degrees centigrade.

P: How far is it from the airport to the downtown?

S: It is not very far, about 25 kilometers.

P: Would you mind telling me how I can go to the hotel from the airport?

S: Which hotel would you like to stay in?

P: I have made a reservation at Yanjing Hotel. Do you know where it is?

S: As I know, no bus goes there directly. You can take a taxi, or the information desk in the terminal building will be able to advise you about public transport. But I would suggest you take the limousine. It is cheaper and just as fast. It will take you downtown and you can take a taxi to the hotel from there.

P: But how can I tell the taxi driver to go to my hotel? I can speak little Chinese.

S: Well, some taxi drivers speak a little English. I will write down the name of your hotel in Chinese on a piece of paper and then you just show it to the taxi driver in case he doesn't understand you. He will take you there, is that OK?

P: That's a good idea. But approximately how much is taxi fare?

S: About 100 RMB.

P: Is there an additional charge for baggage?

S: No, you don't have to pay for it.

P: Do I have to give the taxi driver a tip?

S: It's unnecessary. No tip here.

P: Thanks a lot. You've been very helpful.

S: Do not mention it. Now the passenger ladder has just been put in its position. You can get your belongings ready for disembarkation. Please take the ferry bus when you disembark and it will carry you fight to the arrival hall.

P: Thanks a lot.

S: I hope you have a nice time in Beijing.

S: Is your baggage here, Sir?

P: Yeah. I have everything with me. Thank you so much for everything you have done for me. It has been a comfortable flight.

S: I'm glad you have enjoyed the flight, arid it's a great pleasure for us to be at your service.

P: Well, it's time for me to say goodbye to you.

S: We look forward to serving you again in the future. Goodbye and good luck!

5.1.3   Cultural Background

ICAO—the International Civil Aviation Organization

ICAO—the International Civil Aviation Organization—was established in 1944 by 52 nations whose aim was to assure the safe, orderly and economic development of international air transport. ICAO has its headquarters in Montreal, Canada, with seven regional offices throughout the world. From its beginning it has grown to an organization with over 180 Contracting States. It provides the forum whereby requirements and procedures in need of standardization may be introduced, studied land resolved.

In November 1944, the U.S. government extended an invitation to 55 States or authorities to attend an International Civil Aviation Conference in Chicago. Fifty-four States attended this Conference, and in the end a Convention on International Civil Aviation was signed by 52 States, setting up the permanent International Civil Aviation Organization (ICAO) as a means to secure international co-operation a highest possible degree of uniformity in regulations and standards, procedures and organization regarding civil aviation matters. At the same time the International Services Transit Agreement and the International Air Transport Agreement were signed.

According to the terms of the Convention, the Organization is made up of an Assembly a Council of limited membership with various subordinate bodies and a Secretariat. The chief officers are the President of the Council and the Secretary General.

The Assembly, composed of representatives from all Contracting States, is the sovereign body of ICAO. It meets every three years, reviewing in detail the work of the Organization and setting policy for the coming years. It also votes a triennial budget. The Assembly elects the Council the governing body for a three-year term.

The Council, the governing body which is elected by the Assembly for a three-year term, is composed of 36 States. The Assembly chooses the Council Member States under three headings: States of chief importance in air transport, States which make the largest contribution to the provision of facilities for air navigation, and States whose designation will ensure that all major areas of the world are represented. As the governing body, the Council gives continuing direction to the work of ICAO. It is in the Council that Standards and Recommended Practices, are adopted and incorporated as Annexes to the Convention on International Civil Aviation. The Council is assisted by the Air Navigation Commission (technical matters), the Air Transport Committee (economic matters), the Committee on Joint Support of Air Navigation Services and the Finance Committee.

The Secretariat, headed by a Secretary General, is divided into five main divisions: the Air Navigation Bureau, the Air Transport Bureau, the Technical Co-operation Bureau, the Legal Bureau, and the Bureau of Administration and Services. In order that the work of the Secretariat shall reflect a truly international approach, professional personnel are recruited on a broad geographical basis.

ICAO works in close co-operation with other members of the United Nations family such as the World Meteorological Organization, the International Telecommunication Union, the Universal Postal Union, the World Health Organization and the International Maritime Organization. Non-governmental organizations which also participate in ICAO's work include the International Air Transport Association, the Airports Council International, the International Federation of Air Line Pilots' Associations, and the International Council of Aircraft Owner and Pilot Associations.

5.2　Seeing Special Passengers Off in the Cabin

5.2.1　Language Points and Useful Sentence Patterns

5.2.1.1　Language Points

1. terminal

Station where transport vehicles load or unload passengers or goods.

2. unaccompanied

If someone is unaccompanied, they are alone.

3. document

Writing that provides information.

4. ground staff

The people who are paid to maintain a sports ground are called the ground staff.

5.2.1.2　Useful Sentence Patterns

Seeing Off Jargon

Hope you fly with us again.

Enjoy your stay in Shanghai.

Good-bye and hope to see you again.

Have a good time in Shanghai.

5.2.2　Dialogues

5.2.2.1　Helping disabled passengers

(P: Passenger　S: Stewardess)

S: Excuse me, Sir, please sit down now! Please remain seated until the plane comes to a complete stop. It is very dangerous to open the overhead locker, please turn it off right now.

P: When can we disembark?

S: When the plane comes to a complete stop and the boarding bridge is ready. May I assist you to disembark when ground staff arrives with the wheelchair?

P: Thank you so much, please bring me my crutch. It is in the closet.

S: OK. Would you mind holding my arm? I will take you to the exit.

5.2.2.2　Helping an unaccompanied kid get off the airplane

(P: Passenger　S: Stewardess)

S: Hi honey, it is rather windy outside. You had better put on your overcoat.

P: How far is it to the terminal building? Do I have to walk there?

S: No, you do not. We have transportation down near the aircraft to send you to the terminal building. Please be hurry, or you will Miss the shuttle bus.

P: That is wonderful. I am very satisfied with China eastern airlines next time I will choose china eastern airlines again.

S: It is our pleasure. Let me help you to take your small bag in the overhead compartment. Here is your traveling documents and return ticket, now I give them to the ground staff.

S: Good-bye and hope to see you again.

5.2.2.3　Helping transfer passengers

(P: Passenger　S: Stewardess)

P: Excuse me, Madam. Shanghai is only my transit airport. I want to go to Wuhan. Where should I go now?

S: You may go to the transfer counter at the terminal building to check your reservation.

Have you checked your baggage to your final destination?

P: Yes, I have. My connecting flight is also china eastern airlines, should I bring my checked baggage in shanghai?

S: No, you don't need to bring your checked baggage in Shanghai, and then you can take your connecting flight to Wuhan, and then take your checked baggage in Wuhan directly.

P: All right. Thank you very much.

5.2.2.4   Helping Female Passengers

(P: Passenger   S: Stewardess)

P: Excuse me, Madam, the trunk is so heavy that I cannot put it down from the overhead locker. Could you do me a favor?

S: Yes, it is my pleasure. Oh, the trunk is really too heavy, let us put it down from the overhead locker together.

P: All right. Thank you very much. I am very satisfied with your service, next time I hope to meet you again.

S: Hello, Sir, would you please allow this woman to go first?

P: Yes, of course, Lady first!

S: Thank you. Enjoy your stay in Shanghai. Hope you fly with us again.

P: Excuse me, Madam, my stomach is very painful, is there ginger tea on the plane?

S: Don't worry and I'll make a cup of ginger tea for you right now.

5.2.3   Cultural Background

IATA—The International Air Transport Association

IATA—The International Air Transport Association—was founded in Havana, Cuba, in April 1945. It is the prime vehicle for inter-airline cooperation in promoting safe, reliable, secure and economical air services—for the benefit of the world's consumers. The international scheduled air transport industry is now more than 100 times larger than it was in 1945. Few industries can match the dynamism of that growth, which would have been much less spectacular without the standards, practices and procedures developed within IATA.

The modern IATA is the successor to the International Air Traffic Association founded in Hague in 1919—the year of the world's first international scheduled services. At its founding, IATA had 57 members from 31 nations, mostly in Europe and North America. Today it has some 240 members from 126 nations in every part of the globe.

Over 60 years, IATA has developed the commercial standards that built a global industry. Today, the mission of IATA is to represent, lead and serve the airline industry. Its 240 member airlines—the world's leading passenger and cargo airlines among them—represent 94 percent of scheduled international air traffic.

IATA seeks to improve understanding of the industry among decision makers and increase awareness: of the benefits that aviation brings to national and global economies. It fights for the interests of airlines across the globe 9 challenging unreasonable rules and charges, holding regulators and governments to account, and striving for sensible regulation.

IATA aim is to help airlines help themselves by simplifying processes and increasing passenger convenience while reducing costs and improving efficiency. Moreover, safety is IATA's number one priority and IATA' goal is to continually improve safety standards, notably through IATA's Operational Safety Audit (IOSA). Another main concern is to minimize the impact of air transport on environment.

IATA ensures that people and goods can move around the global airline network as easily as possible if they were on a single airline in a single country. In addition, it provides essential professional support to all industry stakeholders with a wide range of products and expert services, such as publications, training and consulting. IATA's financial systems also help carriers and the travel industry maximize revenues.

5.3   Luggage Counter

5.3.1   Language Points and Useful Sentence Patterns

5.3.1.1   Language Points

1. conveyor belt

Continuously-moving strip of rubber or metal which is used in factories for moving objects along so that they can be dealt with as quickly as possible.

2. urgent

Compelling immediate action.

3. apologize

Acknowledge failings or faults.

4. transportation

Any type of vehicle that you can travel in or carry goods in.

5. lobby

A large entrance or reception room or area.

5.3.1.2   Useful Sentence Patterns

Luggage Counter Jargon

What can I do for you?

What is the matter with you?

Wait a moment please.

Please show me your boarding pass.

Let me check it for you.

5.3.2　Dialogues

5.3.2.1　Baggage Claim

(P: Passenger　　S: Stewardess)

P: Excuse me, Sir.

S: Yes. What can I do for you, Miss?

P: I can't find my baggage on the conveyor belt.

S: Don't worry. Wait a moment, please.

P: All of the baggages have been sent out except mine.

S: What's your luggage?

P: Well, it's a suitcase.

S: Is there any clear sign on your case?

P: It's a big blue case. There is a big sign of my name on it.

S: Look! A big blue case is coming now! Is it yours?

P: Yes. That's mine.

S: OK, let's get a cart and lift your case on it.

P: Thanks a lot. You're so kind.

S: My pleasure. Have a nice trip!

5.3.2.2　Baggage Lost

(P: Passenger　　S: Stewardess)

S: Why are you worried, Sir?

P: I can't find my baggage here. Can you help me?

S: Sure. Have you got your baggage check?

P: Here you are. Could you check it as soon as possible? I have something urgent now.

S: Of course, ma'am. Please wait for a moment while we are investigating.

P: OK, I wait.

S: I'm sorry, Sir. We are not able to locate your baggage yet.

P: Are you kidding? You mean I lost my baggage?

S: Don't worry, Sir. I'll check your luggage information again. Oh… I'm sorry to tell you that your luggage was not loaded on the aircraft.

P: So what could I do?

S: We apologize for that. We'll take responsibility and arrange another flight for transportation. When your baggage arrives, we'll contact you immediately.

P: OK. Please deliver it to Peking Hotel.

S: No problem.

5.3.2.3   Contacting the ground crew

(P: Passenger   S: Stewardess)

P: Excuse me, where can I get back my checked baggage?

S: In the Baggage Claim Area in the arrival lobby.

P: How do I know which conveyor belt to go to? I suppose there must be a lot in such a large airport.

S: Don't worry. You will see signs to the baggage claim. They will tell you which belt the luggage from this flight is on.

P: How can I decide which bag is mine if a few of them look alike.

S: You can easily recognize which one is yours by matching the number on the baggage tag attached to your ticket with that on your bag.

P: Oh, I see. Thank you.

5.3.2.4   Baggage Claim area

(P: Passenger   S: Stewardess)

P: Excuse me, could you tell me where the Baggage Claim Area is? I have got checked baggage but I do not know where the baggage claim area is.

S: The Baggage Claim Area is in the arrival hall. When you arrive, you will see signs to the Baggage Claim Area and Exit. If you follow them you will find your bags.

P: Oh, I have already see my checked baggage. Thank goodness, it turned out to be the first one out.

S: Excuse me, Sir, please show me your boarding pass.

P: Here you are.

S: I am sorry, I think you have make a mistake, this is not your luggage.

P: Oh, really? Let me check the boarding pass, it is not mine, but where is my luggage?

S: Maybe that one is yours, they look like the same.

P: Oh, I see. Thank you so much.

5.3.3   Cultural Background

Airbus SAS

Airbus SAS is a division of the multinational Airbus SE that manufactures civil aircraft. It is based in Blanca, France, a suburb of Toulouse, with production and manufacturing facilities mainly in France, Germany, Spain, China, United Kingdom and the United States. The company employed 72,816 people in 2016.

Airbus began as a consortium of aerospace manufacturers, Airbus Industries. Consolidation of European defense and aerospace companies in 1999 and 2000 allowed the establishment of a simplified joint-stock company in 2001, owned by the European Aeronautic Defense and Space Company (EADS) (80%) and BAE Systems (20%). After a protracted sales process BAE sold its shareholding to EADS on 13 October 2006.

Airbus has sixteen key sites in four countries: France, Germany, Spain and the United Kingdom. Final assembly production is based at Toulouse, France; Hamburg, Germany; Seville, Spain, Tianjin, China, and Mobile, United States. Airbus has subsidiaries in the United States, Japan and India.

The company produces and markets the first commercially viable digital fly-by-wire airliner, the Airbus A320, and the world's largest passenger airliner, the A380. The 10,000th aircraft, an A350, was delivered to Singapore Airlines on 14 October 2016; the global Airbus fleet having performed more than 110 million flights over 215 billion kilometers, carrying 12 billion passengers.

5.4　Passenger Inquiries

5.4.1　Language Points and Useful Sentence Patterns

5.4.1.1　Language Points

1. customs

Money collected under a tariff.

2. declaration

Official announcement or statement.

3. transit

Make a passage or journey from one place to another.

4. apron

A garment of cloth or leather or plastic that is tied about the waist and worn to protect your clothing.

5. shuttle

Badminton equipment consisting of a ball of cork or rubber with a crown of feathers.

5.4.1.2　Useful Sentence Patterns

Answer Passenger Inquiries Jargon

Would you please fill out these forms?

This one is the Incoming Passenger Card.

We have transportation near the aircraft to take you to the terminal building.

You can go to Terminal 2 by free shuttle bus.

5.4.2　Dialogues

5.4.2.1　Immigration Forms

(P: Passenger　S: Stewardess)

S: Excuse me, Sir. We are landing in half an hour. Would you please fill out these forms?

P: What is this white form?

S: This is a Customs Declaration Form. All dutiable articles must be listed in this form.

P: What about this one?

S: This one is the Incoming Passenger Card. You will need it when you go through immigration.

P: Do I have to give them back to you before landing?

S: No, you do not have to. You will need them when you go through your entry.

5.4.2.2　Terminal Transit

(P: Passenger　S: Stewardess)

P: Miss, how far is it to the terminal building? Do we have to walk over there?

S: No, you do not. We have transportation near the aircraft to take you to the terminal building.

P: This is my first time in Taipei, how many terminals are there in Songshan Airport?

S: There are 2 terminals in Songshan Airport, one is for domestic flight, the other one is for international flight. Where is your next destination?

P: My next destination is Gaoxiong. Which terminal should I go?

S: You can go to Terminal 2 by free shuttle bus, then check in at Terminal 2 .

P: Thank you very much .How warm are Taiwanese!

5.4.2.3　Connecting Flight

(P: Passenger　S: Stewardess)

P: Is there any announcement or information for us to get on board?

S: Of course, please listen carefully.

If you continue the flight with us, please obtain your boarding pass from the ground staff and wait for departure in the terminal building.

If you have a connecting flight, you will have to go to the domestic terminal after you have declared customs. It's just beside the international terminal.

P: Why should I leave the plane, I do not want to get off the plane, can I wait on the plane?

S: I'm sorry, Sir, you can not wait on the plane, because we have to clean up the plane for the next flight.

P: How about leave the baggage on the plane?

S: You may leave your baggage on the plane but take valuables and important documents with you. The plane will stop here for one hour and ten minutes.

P: OK, see you later .

5.4.3 Cultural Background

The Boeing Company

The Boeing Company is an American multinational corporation that designs, manufactures, and sells airplanes, rotorcraft, rockets, and satellites worldwide. The company also provides leasing and product support services. Boeing is among the largest global aircraft manufacturers; it is the second-largest defense contractor in the world based on 2015 revenue, and is the largest exporter in the United States by dollar value. Boeing stock is a component of the Dow Jones Industrial Average.

The Boeing Company's corporate headquarters are located in Chicago and the company is led by President and CEO Dennis Muhlenberg. Boeing is organized into five primary divisions: Boeing Commercial Airplanes (BCA); Boeing Defense, Space & Security (BDS); Engineering, Operations & Technology; Boeing Capital; and Boeing Shared Services Group. In 2016, Boeing recorded $94.6 billion in sales, ranked 24th on the Fortune magazine "Fortune 500" list (2017), ranked 61st on the "Fortune Global 500" list (2017), and ranked 30th on the "World's Most Admired Companies" list (2017).

5.5   Airport Service

5.5.1   Language Points and Useful Sentence Patterns

5.5.1.1   Language Points

1. hall

An interior passage or corridor onto which rooms open.

2. cheaper

Relatively low in price or charging low prices.

3. disembark

When passengers disembark from a ship, aeroplane, or bus, they leave it at the end of their journey.

5.5.1.2   Useful Sentence Patterns

Airport Service Jargon

Which hotel would you like to stay in?

It is a great honor for us to be at your service.

We are waiting for the apron shuttle bus to take us to the arrival hall.

5.5.2　Dialogues

5.5.2.1　The convenient and cheap way to city center

(P: Passenger　　S: Stewardess)

P: Excuse me, Miss. Could you tell me how I can get to my reserved hotel in the downtown hotel?

S: Which hotel would you like to stay in?

P: I have made a reservation at Sunny Hotel in the downtown. Do you know where Sunny Hotel is?

S: Yes. As I know, no bus goes there directly. You can hire a taxi right outside the terminal hall. But I would suggest taking the limousine. It is a lot cheaper. It will take you downtown and then you can lake a taxi to Sunny Hotel from there.

P: But how can I tell the taxi driver to go to my hotel?

S: Well, do you have a piece of paper and a pen?

P: Yes, here you are.

A: I will write down the name of the hotel in Chinese and then show it to the taxi driver. He'll take you there, is that OK?

P: That is a good idea. But how much is the taxi fare?

A: About 20 Yuan. And you should make sure there is nothing on the meter before the driver throws the sign.

P: Is there an additional charge for baggage?

S: No. You don't have to pay for it.

P: What is the standard tip these days?

S: No. You don't do that. No tip here.

P: Thanks a lot. You have been very helpful.

S: Do not mention it. Now the air bridge has just been put in its position. You can get your belongings ready for disembarkation. Are you sure nothing is left behind?

P: Yeah. I have everything with me. Thank you so much for everything you have done for me. It has been a comfortable flight.

S: We are glad you have enjoyed the flight and it is a great honor for us to be at your service.

P: Well, it is time for me to say goodbye to you.

A: We look forward to serving you again in the future.

P: It certainly will.

S: Good-Bye! Goodbye and good luck!

P: Goodbye.

5.5.2.2　Shuttle Bus

(P: Passenger　S: Stewardess)

P: Why can not we get off the plane? What are we waiting for?

S: We are waiting for the apron shuttle bus to take us to the arrival hall.

P: What is an apron shuttle bus?

S: It is a transit bus that runs between the parking area of the plane and the arrival hall. So the passengers do not have to walk a long way to the terminal.

P: I used to get to the terminal through an air-bridge. Anyway, I am glad I am back. Good day, Miss.

S: Good day, Sir. Thank you for flying with Air China.

5.5.3　Cultural Background

Airbus

Airbus is in tight competition with Boeing every year for aircraft orders although Airbus has secured over 50% of aircraft orders in the decade since 2003. Airbus won a greater share of orders in 2003 and 2004. In 2005, Airbus achieved 1 111 (1055 net) orders, compared to 1029 (net of 1002) for the same year at rival Boeing. However, Boeing won 55% of 2005 orders proportioned by value; and in the following year Boeing won more orders by both measures. Airbus in 2006 achieved its second best year ever in its entire 35-year history in terms of the number of orders it received, 824, second only to the previous year. Airbus plans to increase production of A320 airliners to reach 40 per month by 2012, at a time when Boeing is increasing monthly 737 productions from 31.5 to 35 per month.

Regarding operational aircraft, there were 7,264 Airbus aircraft operational at April 2013. Although Airbus secured over 50% of aircraft orders in the decade since 2003, the number of Boeing aircraft still in operation at April 2013 still exceeded Airbus by 21% because Airbus made a late entry into the market, 1972 vs. 1958 for Boeing; this lead is diminishing as older aircraft are progressively retired.

Though both manufacturers have a broad product range in various segments from single-aisle to wide-body, their aircraft do not always compete head-to-head. Instead they respond with models slightly smaller or bigger than the other in order to plug any holes in demand and achieve a better edge. The A380, for example, is designed to be larger than the 747. The A350XWB competes with the high end of the 787 and the low end of the 777. The A320 is bigger than the 737-700 but smaller than the 737-800. The A321 is bigger than the 737-900 but smaller than the previous 757-200. Airlines see this as a benefit since they get a more complete product range from 100 seats to 500 seats than if both companies offered identical aircraft.

In recent years the Boeing 777 has outsold its Airbus counterparts, which include the A340 family as well as the A330-300. The smaller A330-200 competes with the 767, outselling its Boeing counterpart in recent years. The A380 is anticipated to further reduce sales of the Boeing 747, gaining Airbus a share of the market in very large aircraft, though frequent delays in the A380 programmed have caused several customers to consider the refreshed 747-8. Airbus has also proposed the A350 XWB to compete with the Boeing 787 Dream liner, after being under great pressure from airlines to produce a competing model.

Airbus will open a R&D center and venture capital fund in Silicon Valley. Airbus CEO Fabric Berger stated: "What is the weakness of a big group like Airbus when we talk about innovation? We believe that we have better ideas than the rest of the world. We believe that we know because we control the technologies and platforms. The world has shown us in the car industry, the space industry and the hi-tech industry that this is not true. And we need to be open to others' ideas and others' innovations."

Airbus Group CEO Tom Enders stated that the only way to do it for big companies is really to create spaces outside of the main business where we allow and where we incentivize experimentation... That is what we have started to do but there is no manual... It is a little bit of trial and error. We all feel challenged by what the Internet companies are doing.

Unit 6
Crew Broadcasting

6.1   Routine Broadcasting

6.1.1   Language Points and Useful Sentence Patterns

6.1.1.1   Language Points

1. airbus

A subsonic jet airliner operated over short distances.

2. fleet

Group of aircraft operating together under the same ownership.

3. luggage

A case used to carry belongings when traveling.

4. compartment

A small space or subdivision for storage.

5. aviation

The aggregation of a country's military aircraft.

6. electronic

Of or relating to electronics; concerned with or using devices that operate on principles governing the behavior of electrons.

7. cooperation

Joint operation or action.

8. alliance

The state of being allied or confederated.

9. precaution

A precautionary measure warding off impending danger or damage or injury etc.

10. Unpredictable

Not capable of being foretold.

11. turbulence

Unstable flow of a liquid or gas.

12. Fahrenheit

Of or relating to a temperature scale proposed by the inventor of the mercury thermometer.

6.1.1.2   Useful Sentence Patterns

Flight Delay Jargon

Our flight will be delayed due to air traffic control.

Our Captain will keep in touch with the tower.

Please wait and we will keep you informed.

Our flight will be delayed due to Mechanical failure.

6.1.2　Broadcasting

6.1.2.1　Boarding

女士们、先生们、亲爱的朋友们：

东方航空欢迎您。

今天您乘坐的是东航最新引进的空中客车 A330-300 型飞机，本次航班从上海飞往北京。

座位号码在行李架下方，请对号入座。请将您的手提物品放在行李架上或座椅下的挡杆区域内，请保持过道和紧急出口畅通。

我们会尽快协助您入座，一起开始今天的旅程。

Good morning, Ladies and Gentlemen:

Welcome aboard China Eastern Airlines, from Shanghai to Beijing. And the aircraft is an Airbus A330-300, the newest member of the China Eastern fleet.

Please make sure your luggage is stored in the overhead compartment or under the seat in front of you. Please keep the aisles and the exits clear.

Thank you for your cooperation!

6.1.2.2　Before Cabin Door Closing

女士们、先生们：

您乘坐的是 MU5101 航班，飞往北京，与达美航空 7001 实施代码共享。

我们马上就要关闭舱门了。

为了飞行安全，请您全程关闭手机电源，直至航班到达后舱门打开。同时在起飞和下降过程中，请不要使用任何电子设备。

谢谢您的协助！

Ladies and Gentlemen:

We will be flying to Beijing. This flight is MU5101, which is code-share with Delta 7001.

The cabin door will be closing shortly.

According to China Civil Aviation Regulation, Mobile phones, even in flight mode, are not permitted to be used during flight. And no electronic device is permitted to be used during take-off and landing.

Thank you for your cooperation!

6.1.2.3　Greetings

（正常航班）

女士们、先生们、"东方万里行"的会员们：

早上好！

欢迎您乘坐天合联盟成员中国东方航空班机。

我是本次航班的客舱经理。我们全体乘务员将竭诚为您服务，希望能给您带来愉快、舒适的旅程。

稍后我们会为您播放安全录像，请您留意观看。

Ladies and Gentlemen, members of Eastern Miles:

Good morning!

Welcome aboard China Eastern Airlines, a member of Sky Team Alliance.

I'm the in-flight service manager.

Today, together with my team members, we will be at your service. We hope to make your journey pleasant and comfortable.

"Safety instructions" video will be played soon.

Your attention will be appreciated.

（延误航班）

女士们、先生们、"东方万里行"的会员们：

早上好！

欢迎您乘坐天合联盟成员中国东方航空班机。

我是本次航班的客舱经理。我谨代表中国东方航空感谢您选择我们的航班。

由于航路交通管制原因，我们还需等待一些时间从本站起飞。我们的机长正在积极与塔台保持联络，如果有进一步的消息，我们会尽快通知您。给您带来不便，我们深表歉意，感谢您的谅解！

稍后我们会为您播放安全录像，请您留意观看。

Ladies and Gentlemen, members of Eastern Miles:

Good morning!

Welcome aboard China Eastern Airlines, a member of Sky Team Alliance.

I'm the in-flight service manager. Today, together with my team members, we will be at your service.

Our flight will be delayed due to air traffic control, our captain will keep in touch with the tower. Please wait and we will keep you informed.

Thank you for your understanding!

"Safety instructions" video will be played soon.

Your attention will be appreciated.

WORDS AND EXPRESSIONS

alliance *n.* the state of being allied or confederated

mile *n.* a unit of length equal to 1760 yards

delayed *adj.* caused to be slower or later

baggage *n.* a case used to carry belongings when traveling

6.1.2.4　Trip Plan

女士们、先生们:

我们已经飞翔在蓝天白云之间。

旅途中您可以使用座椅前的耳机欣赏《暮光之城》《功夫熊猫》和《黑衣人》等影音节目。如果您要使用个人电脑,请记得关闭无线网卡功能。

我们正在为您准备晚餐,稍后您就可以享用了。餐后,我们将销售免税商品。北京时间早上 7 点 30 分,我们还会为您提供早餐。

飞行途中难免会碰到不可预测的颠簸气流,为保证您的安全,请务必始终系好安全带。飞机颠簸时,请不要离开座位。

愿我们能陪伴您度过美好的空中时光。

Ladies and Gentlemen:

We have left Shanghai.

You may use the headset in front seat pocket and enjoy movie such as *Twilight*, *Kung Fu Panda* and *Man in Black*. While using your personal laptop, please make sure the WIFI card has been switched off.

We will soon be serving you dinner. Duty-free sales will begin after the meal service.

And we will serve you breakfast at 7:30 in the morning.

As a precaution against unpredictable clear turbulence, please keep your seat belts fastened while seated and avoid walking about in the cabin when the aircraft is bumpy.

Thank you!

6.1.2.5　Time & Weather & Descending

女士们、先生们:

现在是北京时间 3 点 30 分,当地时间 4 点 30 分。我们的飞机会在 30 分钟后到达东京成田机场。

东京的天气晴朗,地面温度为 25 摄氏度,77 华氏度。

飞机已经开始下降。谢谢您在这段旅途中给我们的支持和帮助。

现在,请您系好安全带,收起小桌板,调直椅背,打开遮光板,确认所有电子设备已关闭。

机上娱乐节目就要结束了,请将耳机放在座椅口袋里。

同时,为了确保下降过程中的安全,请您将行李放置在行李架上或座椅下挡杆区域内。在飞机着陆及滑行期间,请不要开启行李架。稍后,客舱灯光将会调暗,机上洗手间将停止使用。

谢谢!

Ladies and Gentlemen:

It is 3:30 Beijing time and 4:30 local time. We will be landing at Narita International Airport in about 30 minutes. The weather is clear. The ground temperature is 25 degrees Centigrade, and 77 degrees Fahrenheit.

We will be landing soon. Please fasten your seat belt, put tray table to the upright position, and make sure the window shade is open and all electronic devices are switched off.

The entertainment system will be switched off shortly, please put your headphone in the seat pocket.

For your safety, please make sure all your luggage are put in the overhead compartment or under the seat, and do not open the overhead compartment during landing and taxiing.

We will dim the cabin lights shortly, please turn on your reading light if you keep reading. The lavatories will be closing soon.

Thank you!

6.1.2.6 After Landing

女士们、先生们：

欢迎来到上海。现在是北京时间 3 点 30 分，地面温度为 25 摄氏度，77 华氏度。

飞机还在滑行，请不要站起来，保持安全带系好，手机关闭，直到飞机完全停稳、舱门打开。下机前打开行李架时，请您小心，以免行李滑落发生意外。

非常感谢您选择了天合联盟成员中国东方航空。我们全体机组成员祝您一切顺利，期待下次再会。

Ladies and Gentlemen:

Welcome to Shanghai.

It is 3:30 Local Time. The ground temperature is 25 degrees Centigrade or 77 degrees Fahrenheit.

While the aircraft is taxiing, please be seated and remain your seat belt fasten. Please keep your mobile phones powered off until the cabin door is opened. Meanwhile, please pay special attention to falling luggage when you open the overhead compartment after the aircraft has completely stopped.

Thank you for choosing China Eastern Airlines, a member of Sky Team Alliance. On behalf of Miss. Li and her crew, we wish you all the best and look forward to serving you again.

WORDS AND EXPRESSIONS

centigrade *adj.* of or relating to a temperature scale on which the freezing point of water is 0 degrees and the boiling point of water is 100 degrees

taxi *v.* travel slowly

crew *n.* the men who man a ship or aircraft

6.1.3 Cultural Background

Airbus A380

The Airbus A380 is a double-deck, wide-body, four-engine jet airliner manufactured by

European manufacturer Airbus. It is the world's largest passenger airliner, and the airports at which it operates have upgraded facilities to accommodate it. It was initially named Airbus A3XX and designed to challenge Boeing's monopoly in the large-aircraft market. The A380 made its first flight on 27 April 2005 and entered commercial service on 25 October 2007 with Singapore Airlines. An improved version, the A380 plus, is under development.

The A380's upper deck extends along the entire length of the fuselage, with a width equivalent to a wide-body aircraft. This gives the A380-800's cabin 550 square meters (5,920 sq ft) of usable floor space, 40% more than the next largest airliner, the Boeing 747-8, and provides seating for 525 people in a typical three-class configuration or up to 853 people in an all-economy class configuration. The A380-800 has a design range of 8,500 nautical miles (15,700 km), serving the second- and third-longest non-stop scheduled flights in the world (as of February 2017), and a cruising speed of Mach 0.85 (about 900 km/h, 560 mph or 490 km at cruising altitude).

As of May 2017, Airbus had received 317 firm orders and delivered 213 aircraft; Emirates is the biggest A380 customer with 142 ordered of which 97 have been delivered.

6.2   Safety Broadcasting

6.2.1   Language Points and Useful Sentence Patterns

6.2.1.1   Language Points

1. waist

The narrowing of the body between the ribs and hips.

2. locate

Discover the location of; determine the place of; find by searching or examining.

3. buckle

Fastener that fastens together two ends of a belt or strap; often has loose prong.

4. inflate

Fill with gas or air.

5. decompression

Restoring compressed information to its normal form for use or display.

6. elastic

A narrow band of elastic rubber used to hold things (such as papers) together.

7. estimate

An approximate calculation of quantity or degree or worth.

8. securely

In a secure manner; in a manner free from danger.

6.2.1.2　Useful Sentence Patterns

Safety Jargon

For your safety, bring the seatback to the upright position, please.

For your safety, open the window shade, please.

For your safety, fasten your seat belt, please.

For your safety, retune tray table to the upright position, please.

6.2.2　Broadcasting

6.2.2.1　Safety Demonstration

女士们、先生们：

现在我们为您进行客舱安全设备示范，请您注意观看。

Ladies and Gentlemen:

We will now demonstrate the use of the safety equipment on this aircraft. Please give your attention to the crew member at the front of your cabin.

救生衣在您座椅下面。

Your life-vest is located under your seat.

使用时取出，经头部穿好。

To put on the life-vest, slip it over your head.

将带子扣好、系紧。

Fasten the buckle and to tighten it, pull the straps around your waist.

然后，打开充气阀门。

To inflate the life-vest, pull the inflation tab firmly downwards.

但在客舱内请不要充气。

You should inflate your life-vest only at the exit door.

充气不足时，可将救生衣上的人工充气管拉出，用嘴向里充气。

Your life-vest can be further inflated by blowing into the mouth pieces.

氧气面罩储藏在您座椅上方。

The oxygen mask is in the compartment over your head.

当发生客舱释压时，面罩会自动脱落。

In case of decompression, oxygen masks will automatically drop from the compartments above.

氧气面罩脱落后，要用力向下拉面罩。

Pull the mask towards you to start the flow of oxygen.

将面罩罩在口鼻处，带子套在头上，进行正常呼吸。

Place the mask over your nose and mouth, slip the elastic band over your head.

如您的周围有小旅客，请先戴好您的面罩，然后再帮助他。

Masks are available for children. Please attend to yourself first, and then assist your children.

这是您座椅上的安全带。

The seat-belt is on your seat.

使用时，将连接片插入锁扣内。

To fasten your seat-belt, insert the link into the buckle.

根据您的需要，调节安全带的松紧。

To be effective, the seat-belt should be tightly fastened.

解开时，先将锁扣打开，拉出连接片。

To unfasten the seat-belt, lift this buckle.

本架飞机除了正常出口外，在客舱的左右侧还有紧急出口，分别写有紧急出口的明显标志。

Emergency exits are located on each side of the aircraft. All exits are clearly marked.

客舱通道及出口处都设有紧急照明灯，紧急情况下请按指示灯路线撤离飞机。

In an emergency, follow the floor lights to the nearest exits.

安全说明书在您座椅前面的口袋里，请您仔细阅读。

The Safety Instruction Leaflet in your seat pocket contains additional information. Please read it carefully before take-off.

感谢您的关注！

Thank you for your attention!

6.2.2.2　Safety Check

女士们、先生们：

本次航班从上海到北京的飞行距离为 1,146 千米，飞行时间大约需要 1 小时 40 分钟。

飞机已经开始滑行了，请您系好安全带；收起小桌板，调直椅背，打开遮光板，关闭手机等电子设备，包括带有飞行模式功能的手机。

本次航班是禁烟航班，请有吸烟爱好的旅客朋友们理解和支持。

谢谢！

Ladies and Gentlemen:

The flight distance from shanghai to Beijing is 1,146 kilometers, and the estimated flight time is 1 hour and 40 minutes.

Please make sure your seat belt is securely fastened, your tray table and seat back returned to the upright position, keep window shade open, and all mobile phones including in-flight mode and other electronic devices powered off.

Please do not smoke during the whole flight.

Thank you for your cooperation!

6.2.2.3　Before Cabin Door Closing

女士们、先生们：

谢谢您的耐心等待。

飞机很快就要起飞了，请您再次确认安全带已经系好，手机等电子设备已关闭。

谢谢！

Ladies and Gentlemen:

Thank you for your patience.

We will take off shortly, please check your seat belt is securely fastened and keep your mobile phone and other electronic devices switched off.

Thank you.

WORDS AND EXPRESSIONS

securely *adv.* in a secure manner; in a manner free from danger

switch *n.* control consisting of a mechanical or electrical or electronic device for making or breaking or changing the connections in a circuit

6.2.2.4　Seat-Belt Recheck

女士们、先生们：

我们的飞机马上就要降落在北京首都国际机场。

请您再次确认安全带已扣好系紧，所有电子设备已关闭。

谢谢！

Ladies and Gentlemen:

We will be landing at Beijing Capital International Airport shortly.

Please make sure your seat belt is securely fastened and keep your electronic devices switched off.

Thank you!

6.2.3　Cultural Background

C919

The Comac C919 is a narrow-body twinjet airliner developed by Chinese aerospace manufacturer Comac. The programme was launched in 2008 and production of the prototype began in December 2011. It rolled out on 2 November 2015 and first flew on 5 May 2017, for a planned introduction in 2020. The aircraft is mainly made out of aluminum. It is powered by CFM International LEAP turbofan engines and can carry 156 to 168 passengers in a usual operating configuration up to 3,000 nautical miles (5,555 km). It is intended to compete with the Boeing 737 MAX and Airbus A320neo. The last purchase agreement on 13 June 2017 brought the order book to 600 from 24 leasing companies or airlines, mostly Chinese although American engine provider GE has 20 commitments.

The 2008 program launch initially targeted a maiden flight in 2014. Comac applied for a type certificate for the aircraft from the Civil Aviation Authority of China on 28 October 2010. The company intends to manufacture up to 2,300 aircraft of that type. In June 2011, COMAC and Irish low-cost airline Ryan air signed an agreement to co-operate on the development of the C919 In 2012 Airbus' chief strategist Marwan Lahoud was assuming that the aircraft would offer competition to Airbus by 2020.

On 24 November 2011, Comac announced the completion of the joint definition phase, marking the end of the preliminary design phase for the C919, with estimated completion of the detailed design phase in 2012. Production of the first C919 prototype began on 9 December 2011.The C919's aerodynamics were designed with the help of the Tianhe-2 supercomputer. The annual production was targeted at 150 planes by 2020. Bombardier Aerospace has been collaborating since March 2012 on supply chain services, electrical systems, human interface and cockpit; and on flight training, flight-test support, and sales and marketing, from June 2013.

Its announced development budget is 58 billion yuan ($9.5 billion) but its actual cost is estimated at well over $20 billion. The flight tested was expected to complete final assembly in 2014 and perform its first flight in 2015; however, delivery was delayed again until 2018 due to technical difficulties and supply issues. At the November 2014 Zhuhai Air show, it was announced that the first flight would be delayed to 2017. On 2 November 2015, Comac rolled out its first C919 aircraft.

High-speed taxi tests were completed in April 2017 and the first flight took place on 5 May 2017. Comac has a planned test programme of 4,200 flight hours and introduction to service in 2020 with China Eastern Airlines. Slippage into 2021 is possible. The European Aviation Safety Agency is working to validate the Chinese type certificate.

6.3   Emergency Broadcasting

6.3.1   Language Points and Useful Sentence Patterns

6.3.1.1   Language Points

1. suitable

Meant or adapted for an occasion or use.

2. announce

Make known; make an announcement.

3. pick

The person or thing chosen or selected.

4. necktie

Neckwear consisting of a long narrow piece of material worn (mostly by men) under a collar and tied in knot at the front.

5. scarf

A garment worn around the head or neck or shoulders for warmth or decoration.

6. release

Merchandise issued for sale or public showing (especially a record or film).

7. repeat

An event that repeats.

8. demonstration

A show or display; the act of presenting something to sight or view.

9. Confirmation

Additional proof that something that was believed (some fact or hypothesis or theory) is correct.

10. Evacuate

Move out of an unsafe location into safety.

11. relocate

Become established in a new location.

12. appreciate

Recognize with gratitude; be grateful for.

6.3.1.2　Useful Sentence Patterns

Emergency Jargon

Keep clam, that's all right!

Open your seat belt, no baggage, no shoes!

On board, inflate you life vest.

No Exit! Go that side!

6.3.2　Emergency Broadcasting

——机长对旅客广播词：

女士们、先生们：

我是本次航班的机长，现在本架飞机发生——故障，操作困难，决定采取紧急陆地迫降。作为机长，对紧急着陆，我是有信心的，请大家放心，现已经与有关方面联系好，救援人员在等我们。本架飞机全体客舱乘务员经过严格训练，请您听从乘务员的指挥。在着陆时飞机将会有一次或两次冲击。在飞机没有完全停稳前，上体请保持用力状态。谢谢！

Ladies and Gentlemen:

May I have your attention please. This is Captain speaking. Our aircraft has encountered ___ problems and cannot proceed any further, and I decide to make an emergency landing. As an experienced Captain, I'm fully confident to land the aircraft safely. All of your crew members are well trained, for this kind of situation, so please follow instructions from our crew calmly. As there may be a few impacts on touchdown, all passengers should hold upper their bodies until the airplane comes to a full stop. Thank you!

——乘务长对旅客广播词：

女士们、先生们：

　　我是本次航班乘务长，正如机长所述，由于飞机出现不正常情况，为了您的安全，我们将进行水上迫降，迫降后我们将进行应急撤离。现在，我们将进行客舱准备，请听从乘务员的指挥，收起小桌板，调直椅背，打开遮阳板。谢谢！

Ladies and Gentlemen:

This is your chief purser speaking. In preparation for emergency landing, please follow our instructions. Retune seatback and tray table to the upright position and open the window shade.

Thank you!

——广播：

　　为了您疏散时的安全，请松开领口，解下领带、围巾，取下随身携带的尖锐物品，将项链、胸针、钢笔、手镯等放入行李袋内。脱下鞋子交乘务员保管，并穿上外套。

For your safety, please remove all sharp objects, such as necklace, brooch, pen and bracelet. Remove your necktie and scarf. Loose your collar. Remove high-heeled shoes and hand them to your flight attendants. Now, put your coats and jackets on.

——广播：

　　现在乘务员将向您演示救生衣的使用方法，请从座位下取出救生衣，随同乘务员的演示穿上救生衣，但在客舱内不要充气。

Now we will explain the use of life vest. Please take out your life vest and your seat and follow the demonstration of your flight attendants to put it on. But do not inflate it white you are in the cabin.

　　撕开包装，将救生衣经头部穿好，将带子扣好、系紧。

To put the vest on, slip it over your head, then fasten the buckles and pull the straps tight around your waist.

　　当您离开飞机时，拉下救生衣两侧的红色充气把手，但在客舱内不要充气。

Just before leaving the aircraft pull the red tabs to inflate your vest, but do not inflate it while you are in the cabin.

　　充气不足时，可将救生衣上部的人工充气管拉出，用嘴向里充气。

If your vest is not inflated enough, you can also inflate it by blowing into the tubes.

　　乘务员应协助任何需要帮助的旅客穿上救生衣，并清理客舱内救生衣包装袋。

——广播：

　　下面介绍两种防冲撞姿势。

We will now explain two kinds of bracing positions for impact.

第一种：两腿分开，弯下腰，双手用力抓住两脚。如果够不到脚踝，改环抱双膝。

For the first method, put your legs apart, bend over and grab your ankles. If you cannot grab your ankles, grab your knees.

第二种：两腿分开，两臂交叉，身体前倾，双手抓住前面的座椅靠背，额头靠在手臂上。

For the second method, put your legs apart and cross your arms. Hold the seatback and put your forehead on your arms.

当您听到"低下头，紧迫用力"的口令时采取这种防冲击姿势，直到您听到"解开安全带"口令为止。

Take one of bracing positions for emergency impact when the captain orders or when hear "Bend Down" and remain in this position until you hear "open your seat belt".

如果您还有疑问，请向邻座的旅客询问或阅读安全须知。

If you do not understand well, ask your neighbors or read the safety instructions.

——广播：

如果您是民航职员、军人、警察或消防人员，请与我们联系，我们需要您的帮助。同时，我们将调整部分座位，以便帮助需要协助的旅客撤离。

We need helpers, please contact us if you want to be volunteer. We will move some passengers to another section who might need help.

——广播：

本架飞机共有八个应急出口，分别在客舱的前部、后部和中部，并标有紧急出口的明显标志，安装在地板上的紧急灯光将引导您到出口处，白色为撤离路径灯，红色为出口指示灯，撤离时，不准携带任何物品，现在乘务员将告诉您最近出口的位置，请确认至少两个以上的出口。

Attention please! There are eight emergency exits in the cabin, two in the front, two in the rear, four in the middle, and all exits are clearly marked, the track light on the floor will lead you to those exits, leave everything while evacuating, now we will show you the location of your nearest exits.

——广播：

现在，请您取下眼镜、假牙、助听器等放在外衣口袋里，将安全带系得低而紧，做好防冲撞姿势准备，当听到口令"弯腰不动"或"准备冲撞"时，请全身紧迫用力，直到听到"解开安全带"口令为止。注意！撤离必须听从机组成员指挥！

Please put glasses, denture and deaf-aid in your jacket pocket and fasten your seat belt tight and low. You can take one of bracing positions for emergency impact when the captain orders or when hear "Bend Down" and remain in this position until you hear "open your seat belt". Please do follow our instructions when evacuation!

——口令参考：

- 可用出口口令："解开安全带！不要带行李！脱下鞋子！（Open your seat belt, no

baggage, no shoes!）"; "上筏，救生衣充气"（on board inflate you life vest）;

● 不可用出口口令："出口不通！到对面/前面/对面"（No Exit! Go that side / Forward / backward）。

6.3.3　Cultural Background

Boeing 787

The Boeing 787 Dream liner is an American long-haul, mid-size wide body, twin-engine jet airliner made by Boeing Commercial Airplanes. Its variants seat 242 to 335 passengers in typical three-class seating configurations. It is the first airliner with the use of composite materials as the primary material in the construction of its airframe. The 787 was designed to be 20% more fuel efficient than the Boeing 767, which it was intended to replace. The 787 Dream liner's distinguishing features include mostly electrical flight systems, raked wingtips, and noise-reducing chevrons on its engine nacelles. It shares a common type rating with the larger Boeing 777 to allow qualified pilots to operate both models.

The aircraft's initial designation was the 7E7, prior to its renaming in January 2005. The first 787 was unveiled in a roll-out ceremony on July 8, 2007 at Boeing's Everett factory. Development and production of the 787 has involved a large-scale collaboration with numerous suppliers worldwide. Final assembly takes place at the Boeing Everett Factory in Everett, Washington, and at the Boeing South Carolina factory in North Charleston, South Carolina. Originally planned to enter service in May 2008, the project experienced multiple delays. The airliner's maiden flight took place on December 15, 2009, and completed flight testing in mid-2011. Boeing has reportedly spent $32 billion on the 787 program.

Final US Federal Aviation Administration (FAA) and European Aviation Safety Agency (EASA) type certification was received in August 2011 and the first 787-8 was delivered in September 2011. It entered commercial service on October 26, 2011 with launch customer All Nippon Airways. The stretched 787-9 variant, which is 20 feet (6.1 m) longer and can fly 450 nautical miles (830 km) farther than the 787-8, first flew in September 2013. Deliveries of the 787-9 began in July 2014; it entered commercial service on August 7, 2014 with All Nippon Airways, with 787-9 launch customer Air New Zealand following two days later. As of May 2017, the 787 had orders for 1,223 aircraft from 65 customers, with All Nippon Airways having the largest number on order.

The aircraft has suffered from several in-service problems, including fires on board related to its lithium-ion batteries. These systems were reviewed by both the FAA and the Japan Civil Aviation Bureau. The FAA issued a directive in January 2013 that grounded all 787s in the US and other civil aviation authorities followed suit. After Boeing completed tests on a revised battery design, the FAA approved the revised design and lifted the grounding in April 2013; the 787 returned to passenger service later that month.

References

［1］黎富玉. 民航空乘英语［M］. 北京：北京大学出版社，2008.

［2］《民航乘务英语》教材编写组. 民航乘务英语［M］. 北京：高等教育出版社，2006.

［3］林扬，余明洋. 民航乘务英语视听［M］. 北京：旅游教育出版社，2014.

［4］林扬. 民航乘务英语会话［M］. 4 版. 北京：旅游教育出版社，2017.

［5］范建一. 民航乘务英语实用会话［M］. 北京：中国民航出版社，2004.

［6］俞涛. 民航服务英语［M］. 北京：中国民航出版社，2011.

［7］吴啸华，何蕾. 民航服务英语［M］. 北京：国防工业出版社，2017.

［8］尹静. 民航地勤英语［M］. 北京：北京大学出版社，2008.

［9］蒋焕新. 民航地勤服务英语［M］. 北京：科学出版社，2017.

［10］王远梅. 空乘英语［M］. 北京：国防工业出版社，2010.

［11］谢金艳，老青. 空乘及旅游英语视听说［M］. 北京：北京语言大学出版社，2014.

［12］何志强. 民航客舱乘务英语［M］. 北京：中国民航出版社，2015.

［13］林扬. 民航乘务英语会话［M］. 北京：旅游教育出版社，2007.

［14］王晶，余明洋. 民航乘务英语听力［M］. 北京：国防工业出版社，2009.

［15］孙艳芬，孙楠楠. 民航服务英语［M］. 北京：高等教育出版社，2007.

［16］张力，刘茗翀. 民用航空实务英语［M］. 北京：清华大学出版社，2016.